¡cocinando!

TO MY BELOVED MARGOT, ISAAC, AND NONA, WHO KEEP THE HOME FIRES BURNING. AND TO MY FOUR WONDERFUL PARENTS AND MY SPECIAL MOTHER-IN-LAW FOR NURTURING AND SUPPORTING ME THROUGHOUT THE YEARS, ESPECIALLY MY FATHER LUIS WHO WAS THE ROOT INSPIRATION FOR THIS BOOK. A SHOUT OUT AS WELL TO MY BROTHER THEO FOR OUR MUTUAL INTEREST IN MUSIC. AND TO THE DESIGNERS, ARTISTS, MUSICIANS, PRODUCERS, SCHOLARS, AND COLLECTORS WHO HELPED ME ALONG THE WAY, I COULDN'T HAVE DONE IT WITHOUT YOU. I WOULD ALSO LIKE TO DEDICATE THIS BOOK TO THE RECENTLY DECEASED HOLY TRINITY OF CELIA, MONGO, AND COMPAY. MAY THEY KEEP HEAVEN COOKIN'. IN MEMORY OF COUSIN HARRY KOENIGSBURG OF PARIS, TEXAS AND NEW YORK CITY, WHO LOVED THE MAMBO, SAMBA AND THE CHA CHA CHA, SUPPORTED MY ART, AND WAS A DOUBLE FOR TITO PUENTE.

¡Cocinando!

Fifty Years of Latin Album Cover Art

PABLO ELLICOTT YGLESIAS
FOREWORD BY IZZY SANABRIA

PRINCETON ARCHITECTURAL PRESS

NEW YORK

PUBLISHED BY
PRINCETON ARCHITECTURAL PRESS
37 EAST SEVENTH STREET
NEW YORK, NEW YORK 10003

FOR A FREE CATALOG OF BOOKS, CALL 1.800.722.6657.
VISIT OUR WEB SITE AT WWW.PAPRESS.COM.

© 2005 PRINCETON ARCHITECTURAL PRESS
ALL RIGHTS RESERVED
PRINTED AND BOUND IN CHINA
08 07 06 05 5 4 3 2 1 FIRST EDITION

NO PART OF THIS BOOK MAY BE USED OR REPRODUCED IN ANY MANNER WITHOUT WRITTEN PERMISSION FROM THE PUBLISHER, EXCEPT IN THE CONTEXT OF REVIEWS.

EVERY REASONABLE ATTEMPT HAS BEEN MADE TO IDENTIFY OWNERS OF COPYRIGHT. ERRORS OR OMISSIONS WILL BE CORRECTED IN SUBSEQUENT EDITIONS.

PROJECT EDITOR: MARK LAMSTER
ASSISTANT EDITOR: SCOTT TENNENT
DESIGN: DEB WOOD

SPECIAL THANKS TO: NETTIE ALJIAN, NICOLA BEDNAREK, JANET BEHNING, MEGAN CAREY, PENNY (YUEN PIK) CHU, RUSSELL FERNANDEZ, JAN HAUX, CLARE JACOBSON, JOHN KING, NANCY EKLUND LATER, LINDA LEE, JOHN MCGILL, KATHARINE MYERS, JANE SHEINMAN, JENNIFER THOMPSON AND JOSEPH WESTON OF PRINCETON ARCHITECTURAL PRESS
—KEVIN C. LIPPERT, PUBLISHER

LIBRARY OF CONGRESS CATALOGING-IN-PUBLICATION DATA

YGLESIAS, PABLO ELLICOTT, 1964-
  COCINANDO : FIFTY YEARS OF LATIN ALBUM COVER ART / PABLO ELLICOTT YGLESIAS.
    P. CM.
  INCLUDES BIBLIOGRAPHICAL REFERENCES AND INDEX.
  ISBN 1-56898-460-X (ALK. PAPER)
  1. SOUND RECORDINGS—ALBUM COVERS—UNITED STATES.
  2. POPULAR MUSIC—UNITED STATES—HISTORY AND CRITICISM. 3. POPULAR MUSIC—LATIN AMERICA—HISTORY AND CRITICISM. I. TITLE.

NC1883.U6Y49 2004
741.6'6'09045—DC22
                                          2004006366

Contents

FOREWORD: IZZY SANABRIA............ 6
INTRODUCTION..................... 7

MAMBO MANIA.................... 14
CUBOP......................... 42
ORIZA......................... 60
VIVA SOUL..................... 82
ÉCHALE SALSITA................ 112
OYE COMO VA................... 150
OH, MEU BRASIL................ 170
BARRIO NUEVO.................. 200

DISCOGRAPHY...................... 230
BIBLIOGRAPHY..................... 237
ACKNOWLEDGMENTS.................. 238
CREDITS.......................... 239

FOREWORD

IZZY SANABRIA

One evening about a year ago I received a phone call from a young graphic designer and DJ named Pablo Yglesias, who told me he was working on a history of Latin music album covers and that I was to be a big part of the book. I was flattered, but I'd heard it all before. I thought to myself, "Just another well-meaning fan with big ideas." But Pablo was so enthusiastic and persistent that I agreed to meet him in person. I was quickly impressed by his knowledge and understanding of my work and that of my peers—the early pioneers of Latin music album cover design. Hell, the kid knew more about my album cover art than I did. Being a graphic designer himself, as well as a DJ, Pablo seemed the perfect person to pull off this ambitious project.

At a time when CD covers are being produced on computer, the handwork crafted for Latin music covers of the 1960s and 1970s is now rightfully considered and recognized as an art form, or at least as "Latino Pop Art." For early LP designers like Ely Besalel, Abel Navarro, Walter Velez, and myself, it is a matter of great pride to have our work reproduced in a book, and to be applauded for our endeavors in giving Latin music its visual identity. It is especially gratifying that the recognition comes from a fellow Latino artist of a younger generation.

Setting aside the personal glory now being bestowed upon us in our golden years, there is a much greater significance to this book. For the first time the commercial art created for Latin music is being documented for its visual as well as sociological contribution to our music and culture. Pablo covers a lot of ground in this book both before and after my heyday, as well as the work of Brazilian artists. Just as the great works of art reflect social, religious, and political views at different periods of history, these covers reflect fifty years of Latin cultural history through the lens of our music. The covers created in New York during the 1960s and 1970s, for example, helped define Nuyorican culture before it came to the attention of television, film, and print media. This book should not only be pleasing to the eye, but provoke questions about the nature of Latin culture and identity. Through it, future generations of artists will have an opportunity to appreciate, learn from, and perhaps even be influenced by our craftsmanship and creativity.

Am I flattered and thrilled to be a part of this book? Damn right. Am I proud? Absolutely. To those Latinos picking up this book, I hope you will share my pride. If you're a non-Latino, I hope and expect that this book will shed some light on this small part of our visual and commercial culture.

INTRODUCTION

DELUXE: A BRIEF HISTORY OF THE LATIN RECORD COVER

> Our aesthetic forces you to deal with being simultaneously enlightened and offended. It displays a keen sensitivity to universal fears, fantasies, frustrations, and stupidities. In essence, Raunch and Taste. —Walter Velez

I can still clearly recall my first trip, twenty-five years ago, to Record Mart, that bazaar of Latin music down in the throbbing womb of Manhattan's Times Square subway station. Sinuous syncopations coming from that urban oasis echoed along white tiled halls empty of commuters. In the window was a display of albums from the hottest Latin labels: Seeco, Tico, Alegre, Fania, Cotique, Vaya, and Coco.

As a young artist with a love of music, I was immediately drawn to these dazzling records with their swirling worlds of conga and trombone, flamboyant brown-skinned dancers, and swaggering bandleaders. Images of vibrant joy and surrealist fantasy hung alongside troubling images of urban decay and outlaw criminality. I wanted to know the story behind each cover, and I wanted to hear the sounds seductively packaged within. The art set me up, suckering me into buying albums I couldn't afford.

Down in those subterranean record stacks full of mambo and cha cha cha, I was reminded of my father's wild tales of Cuba before Castro, and of his treasure trove of old and abused Latin records. Those LPs came with him on one of the last planes out of Havana on the eve of its fall, in 1959. Thumbing through the folkloric LPs in Record Mart, I also recalled living on the island of Vieques as a child, and of later light-filled adventures to Puerto Rico and Mexico with my mother. Back in those days we listened religiously to the Latino radio program ¿Qué Tal, Amigos? in our Boston kitchen. Those early experiences naturally fueled my decision to become a visual artist and graphic designer and my obsession with the playing and collecting of Latin records.

Years later, I noticed that names like Sanabria, Besalel, Velez, Levine, and Rosario kept popping up in the design credits of my favorite Nuyorican (New York Puerto Rican) album covers. Soon enough, it occurred to me that these unsung heroes and their art warranted serious attention. This book is a product of those investigations, which began innocently enough but eventually developed into a cause.

Latin music, and the design that presents it, is a unique collision of influences: Caribbean, African, European, Indigenous, American. The title of this book, ¡Cocinando!, literally "cooking," seems a perfect metaphor for this inventive cultural stew. But cocinando and salsa—not to mention other words like sabor (flavor) and azúcar (sugar)—mean so much more: sustenance, sensual pleasures, and more importantly, creation, alchemy, identity. As Felipe Luciano declares on the back of Ray Barretto's classic 1972 LP Que viva *la música* (which features the monster cut "Cocinando"): "*Que viva la música* [Long live music]. By any means necessary. Without our music we die. Slowly. Like babies without milk."

When marketing a product to a specific demographic, the idea of identity often becomes a central theme. The sale of Latin music is no exception, and it seemed logical to concentrate on this aspect when planning this book. Album art should be seen not as a mute, ephemeral commodity enslaved to the demands of the music bursting within, but rather as a window onto a culture's evolution, identity, and inner dynamics. What emerges from looking at fifty years of Latin music packaging is the sense that a growing consciousness of self over time was integral to shaping a continually maturing and ever more vital commercial culture. Latin album covers became more powerful and artistically challenging as their imagery moved away from an outsider view of Latino culture as titillating, threatening, and hopelessly exotic toward a native identity that is more in control of its destiny—sometimes honest, sometimes playful and irreverent, but almost always self-created. Throughout, there has been a constant tension and dialog between expressions both high and low, realistic and fantastic, tasty and bland, trashy and sexy, North and South American, exotic and native, retro and contemporary, no-budget and over-budget, and racist and ethnically neutral. In addition to investigating representations of identity, *¡Cocinando!* places Latin music packaging within the historical context of the mainstream realm of graphic design studies hitherto closed to this subject. It is by no means a definitive or comprehensive catalog of Latin album covers. Indeed, there are many gaps and the reader will note a heavy emphasis on the New York and Brazilian Latin music industries.

Latin stereotypes were embodied in early films, music, and literature, giving us such archetypes as the Latin Lover (Rudolph Valentino) and the Street Punk (*West Side Story*). By the 1950s, Latinos made it into America's living rooms in the domesticated machismo and racial miscegenation of *I Love Lucy* and the trickster antics of *Speedy Gonzalez*. From Marlon Brando to Jack Kerouac, every hepcat seemed to own a pair of bongos.

By the mid-1960s, Baby Boomers were humming along to "La Bamba" and "Guantanamera" (sometimes disguised as "Twist & Shout" and "Hang on Sloopy"). Self-proclaimed groovy people dug the Americanized sounds on Tijuana Brass and Brazil '66 records. Cultural stereotypes still clung to Hollywood, but youth of all ethnicities were being increasingly exposed to each other's music and customs. At the close of the decade, the Woodstock generation tripped to the profoundly hybrid sounds of Santana, whose influential album covers were as arresting and revolutionary, in their own way, as his music.

Album covers provide us with a visual companion to the evolving soundtrack of Latin identity. Contrast, for instance, the exotic kitsch of Carmen Miranda's fruit bowl headdress from the 1940s with the cool intellectualism of the Getz/Gilberto covers for Verve in the 1960s. Domestic visions of the Latin "other" had indeed come a long way in just twenty years.

As in mainstream American culture, the massive sociopolitical upheavals and expanding consciousness of the late 1960s sparked a change in perceptions of Latino identity, and by association its manifestation in music packaging. Modern Latin music as we know it starts here with Santana on the West Coast and Willie Colón on the East. New York marketing pioneers like Gabriel Oller, José Curbelo, Izzy Sanabria, Ralph Mercado, and Jerry Masucci worked from within the Latino community to take back a culture that had until then been portrayed through a media controlled by Anglos and their stereotypes, from the outside looking in. It was an uphill battle sometimes: even in the more enlightened 1970s, sexism, machismo, and male-dominated viewpoints often won out. Album covers like Bobby Valentin's *Se la comió* and Colón's *Cosa nuestra* (not to mention TV shows like *Chico and the Man*) did not necessarily help. As in all aspects of creative endeavor, no matter what a person's ethnicity or politics, the tension between the (sometimes mutually exclusive) poles of commercial and artistic impulse are constantly at play in album cover design.

It's fitting to begin talking about Latin music aesthetics with a definition of a slippery term coined in the busy offices of *Latin N.Y.* magazine in the early 1970s. "Deluxe" (pronounced *dee-lux*) seemed to be a useful term when talking about a prevalent look of that period. "Everyone seemed to use it with their own kind of abstract meaning, anything from good to bad to excellent, but generally [denoting] in bad taste but well executed," wrote publisher/editor Izzy Sanabria in the twelfth anniversary edition of the magazine (an issue dedicated to art). "Certain uptight Latinos criticized us for being too cartoony, comic book-ish, and bubble gum, they felt these graphics were not sophisticated enough and created a negative immature image of Latinos," In that same issue, artist and designer Walter Velez countered that "in order to save time and money [Sanabria] created a format that suffered in design quality [but brought] back the old tradition of craftsmanship. To us, normal is only relevant to personal taste, so our Interpretation of 'deluxe' is the very best of the very worst. Deluxe is not malicious, only offensive. It is only offensive to those who can't face themselves, for 'deluxe' is merely a caricature of the human dilemma." Hector Rivera's 1974 album *Lo máximo*, designed by Sanabria with an illustration by Velez, shows the deluxe style at its campy height.

As the deluxe aesthetic came to dominate Latin music graphics, an informal counter-movement developed—ironically spearheaded by Sanabria—with the aim of raising the status of Latino music packaging. The string of covers Sanabria designed for Ray Barretto in the 1970s represent this new, arty direction. In that period, Sanabria boldly grouped primarily Caribbean-derived, East Coast Latin music under an easy-to-use, familiar, and eminently marketable term: *salsa*. The format was soon being promoted intensely, and its success was inextricably linked to album design. Sanabria also took over *Latin N.Y.* (first published in 1968 by artist Peter Rios) in 1973, and overhauled it. With the help of advertising dollars from Jerry Masucci's Fania Records, Sanabria raised production values and created a quality forum for discussion of Latino issues and culture. The revamped *Latin N.Y.* served as a training ground and clearing house for budding talent, inspiring a sense of capability and pride in its readership while spawning important media events like the 1975 *Latin N.Y.* Music Awards and the 1973 TV show *Salsa*, el Barrio's answer to *Soul Train*.

The efflorescence of Nuyorican creativity during the 1960s and early 1970s centered around self-generated projects in the arts and media, bringing people in the community their own radio, theater, art, television, and publications for the first time on a large scale. Masucci produced several feature-length films spotlighting Latin music and culture. In 1973, Larry Harlow and Jenaro Alvarez took a pioneering "latin opera" concept album—*Hommy*, about a blind conga-playing *boricua*—to the stage. Nuyorican authors, poets, playwrights, and visual artists like Piri Thomas, Felipe Luciano, Miguel Piñero, Miguel Algarin, Pedro Pietri, and Papo Colo combined pride and challenging ideas to forge a new form of creative expression in an often divisive and hostile atmosphere. Musically, artists such as Willie Colón, Eddie Palmieri, Ray Barretto, and Rubén Blades were pushing the boundaries of the very music they had forged in the aftermath of the 1960s and the death of Boogaloo and Latin Soul. Initially makeshift (later institutionalized) spaces including Taller Boricua, the Nuyorican Poets Cafe, the New Rican Village, the Hostos Center, El Museo del Barrio, as well as *casitas* like Rincón Criollo and schools like the Boys Harbor Performing Arts Center contributed to an atmosphere of cultural support amidst the decay and neglect of New York's urban battlegrounds. Political awareness and protest also began in earnest, the most committed, vocal, and visible practitioner being the activist Felipe Luciano.

These sociopolitical developments were paralleled on the West Coast by the rise of Chicano culture in the arts, politics, and mass media. Cesar Chavez, the Brown Berets, the Justicia movement, Corky Gonzalez, Ruben Guevara, Oscar "Zeta" Acosta (the original Dr. Gonzo), and comedian Cheech Marin fought stereotypes and oppression with political action, social programs, and satirical humor, bringing to the people of *la raza* both a new self-awareness and a more public sense of ethnic pride. These leaders took social injustices and civil rights issues to the fore just as their African-American compatriots had in the previous decade. At the same time, Chicano artists and musicians became more conscious of their roots and heritage, though perhaps not as politically engaged as their East Coast compatriots. Groups like Malo, Tierra, El Chicano, and Azteca demonstrated an exciting renaissance and re-Latinization process, in turn expanding notions of identity to encompass a pan-Latin agenda and artistic palette. Santana's influence was felt on sympathetic bands like the bi-coastal part-Latino collective Mandrill and the predominantly black band War, from L.A.'s Watts neighborhood.

As the heady creative days of the 1970s progressed toward the resurgent conservatism of the 1980s, the newly self-minted Latino identity began its move into America's broad pop culture, cementing itself firmly in place by the 1990s. Salsa went mainstream with massive concerts and increased radio and TV exposure. Its more *típico* elements were softened with the introduction of a new and slickly polished subgenre, *salsa romantica*. The industry's major labels finally took notice that Latin culture was not operating on the margins of society, that its music was something more than an ethnic genre niche with little commercial potential.

But what of the graphic design used to promote the music? Sadly, many of the visionary pioneers behind the presentation of Latin music in the United States are today unsung, known only to a few within the industry. A roll call of those designers, artists, and photographers would have to include prime innovators like Sanabria and Velez, along with Ely Besalel, Abel Navarro, Warren Flagler, John Murello, Marty Topp, Lee Marshall, and Ron Levine. Following in their footsteps were Charlie Rosario, Jorge Vargas, Yogi Rosario, Manny Vega, Joe Wippler, Victor Diaz, Chico Alvarez, Dominique, Drago, Alan Rodriguez, Angelo Velazquez, Francis Melendez, and Steve Quintana. In some cases, these artists not only developed broad graphic programs, but also helped to position the music intellectually by lending creative album titles, forging identities for musicians, and stretching what was seen as acceptable for the representation of Latin culture. Producers and label presidents like Al Santiago, George Goldner, Ralph Lew, Pancho Cristal, Joe Cain, Jerry Masucci, and Harvey Averne were instrumental in the move to elevate the quality of their covers. And the musicians themselves often participated in the process, sowing the seeds of an idea given by a fan or in an echo from a song.

The blossoming of American Latino album cover art in the late 1960s was a direct outcome of the new sense of creative control experienced by these professionals. Their work was increasingly used to tell stories, to present an overtly artistic message (sometimes spiritual, occasionally political, often satirical or humorous) that represented the music on the inside, instead of serving the merely perfunctory purpose of documentation. Mainstream labels like Columbia, United Artists, and Atlantic followed the independents' lead, marketing already bi-cultural acts like Mongo Santamaría, Willie Bobo, and Santana to a crossover audience and treating visual presentation accordingly.

These covers, from what we might call the Golden Age of Latin music, did not rely on the crutch of "cult of personality" photos (banal but flattering star portraits), an easy formula that would become sadly commonplace in the 1980s.

From an aesthetic standpoint, Latin album cover art has never again reached the heights of this classic period. There are many reasons for blame: the shrunken canvas that is the CD booklet; the immense pressures of crossover success; the insidious, lowest-common-denominator aesthetics of mainstream marketing campaigns; the ever decreasing bottom lines of bloated companies trying to maximize profit on shrinking returns; bootlegging, file sharing, and piracy of all kinds; and the endemic corporate takeover and co-opting of once independent record labels.

Drawing a potential buyer in through cover art alone has become a nearly impossible task. Last ditch efforts include, as design historian Christopher Dunn has noted, "the striking tendency since the 1980s to feature sex[ist] [pinup shots] of nubile women in string bikinis as eye candy for the male consumer"—a consumer who is no doubt overloaded with choices at today's point of purchase. Some labels (especially in the UK and Japan) endeavor to produce quality cover art that retains the standards set by the pioneering artists of the 1960s and 1970s. Some re-issues eschew original cover art in lieu of a slicker, cheaper, or more "contemporary" look, while others skillfully employ a retro style echoing classic designs. Though jazz, world, and rock packaging still exhibit, at least occasionally, innovative or interesting design, Latin music seems to have been in a prolonged slump with only a few bright exceptions.

The story of Brazilian music and its visual presentation provides an interesting counterpoint that parallels that of the U.S. Latin market but differs in several significant ways. The basic roots of Brazilian culture are similar to those of Spanish-speaking New World cultures (particularly in the Caribbean) in that they feature the dynamic intermingling of Iberian, African, and indigenous strains tempered by the lingering effects of colonialism. The impact of centuries of slavery, genocide, forced acculturation, and endemic poverty coupled with the dominance of the ruling oligarchy, the military, and aggressive global finance and industry cannot be underestimated. In visual terms, this commingled history translates into a culturally rich bed of invention, appropriation, and synthesis that often subverts these repressive forces.

Despite these similarities with the Hispanic experience, modern Brazilian music and art is often more intellectualized, and is all the more miraculous for having come of age during a period of intense repression unlike any the Nuyoricans may have experienced in the U.S. Over the past century, Brazilian artistic expression has been informed by the sometimes opposed but often mutually invigorating strains of popular and avant garde culture. Brazil's tradition of domestic vanguardism informed the arts in general, and the country's music and music packaging in particular. Strategies for addressing notions of exoticism and authenticity developed in the 1950s and 1960s among the nation's artists and intellectuals. But as the military coup of 1964 hardened into a repressive, reactionary regime during the late 1960s, artistic expression became increasingly more difficult. In response to the worsening situation and influenced by similar movements around the globe, Brazilian intellectuals, student activists, and emerging young artists catalyzed a major cultural shift. Although united in their opposition to the regime, members of the political left and the cosmopolitan artistic vanguard fought bitterly among themselves, leading to an increasingly radicalized opposition between experimentalism and political engagement, participation and alienation, nationalism and internationalism. São Paulo and Rio de Janeiro enjoyed a brief, prolific flowering of conceptual and interactive art and music, experimental theater, and film.

Musically, the central figures in this renaissance were Gilberto Gil, Caetano Veloso, Tom Zé, Jorge Ben, Maria Bethânia, Os Mutantes, and Gal Costa. The artists/intellectuals Rogério Duarte and Hélio Oiticica inspired this group with their new ideas and produced album covers for their records. Veloso and Gil took the term *tropicalism,* which they borrowed from Oiticica's art installation *Tropicália* (1966–67), to describe their music, a "free" and "all inclusive" sound blending Jimi Hendrix and the Beatles, concrete poetry, found sounds and electronics, and Brazilian music of all genres. The aesthetics of tropicália seemed to promulgate a far-reaching cultural cannibalism, a mixed use of kitsch and pastiche, irony and sincerity, simultaneously looking to the past and streaking into the future in a thoroughly postmodern way. Though earlier musical forms (*bossa nova, jovem garda*, and *iêiêiê*) had broken with tradition and authority, it was not until the counterculture begot the "universal sound" of tropicália that the graphic representation of this music was truly transformed.

By 1970 many young Brazilian artists had been aggressively compromised, silenced, or forced underground by the regime through censorship, intimidation, arrest, incarceration, torture, or exile. Their lyrics and album art of necessity had to subtly code any critiques of the regime. There would be no great mass festivals for Brazil's "Woodstock Generation," but their countercultural attitudes and rigorous aesthetic vision did reverberate, reaching American fans in the 1980s thanks in part to dedicated American musicians and timely compilations.

The aesthetics of early Cuban covers share many of the traits that exemplified other Latin albums of the period: low production values and plenty of racial stereotyping. The revolution, however, led to a crucial break with the past, a break that bears some resemblance to the dramatic changes in the Brazilian and American scenes that occurred in the late 1960s and early 1970s. Of course, there is one crucial difference: in Cuba, the break with the past was sponsored by the state.

Cuban music in the 1960s, like every other aspect of its culture and economy, developed with little U.S. contact, having switched from the American to the Soviet teat. In spite (or perhaps because) of this, a strong graphic art scene developed as part of Castro's political propaganda machine. On the one hand, some Eastern European influence was felt; on the other, an emphasis was placed on promoting self-sufficiency and pride in indigenous culture. There were many limitations on artists and designers, not the least of which were (and remain) a severe lack of materials and a restriction on creative freedom. In response, Cuba's graphic artists were forced to do more with less and to insert hidden messages in their imagery. As expatriate Cuban designer Félix Beltrán has written, "Castro got together with all Cuba's intellectuals and said 'Within the revolution everything is possible, outside of it, nothing.' This was directed to all the artists—painters, sculptors, musicians, dancers, and writers. Everything was permitted as long as there was not an attempt against the revolution. Since the revolution was not immaculate, and had its abuses and contradictions, this message became a straight jacket." Presented here are some of the more nimble attempts to work within Castro's restrictive system.

Corporate America has a way of mass-marketing the trappings of revolution, sucking out the original meaning and threat, and then selling it as either creation myth or canonical history. Drive to a mall in the American Midwest and you'll find kids eating at McDonald's wearing Che Guevara t-shirts. Those kids, and others like them around the world, are drawn to the pop aspects of Latin culture, from crossover success stories like Gloria Estefán, Jennifer Lopez, Ricky Martin, Christina Aguilera, and Marc Anthony, to movie stars like Antonio Banderas, Salma Hayek, and Benicio Del Toro. Leaving its nurturing NPR nest behind, the phenomenon that is the Buena Vista Social Club cut through the palm-tree curtain to bring *el Otro* into mainstream living rooms around the world. Meanwhile, the films of Leon Ichaso, the poetry of Martín Espada, the art of Pepón Osorio, and the music of Conjunto Céspedes—among many others—provide an antidote to some of the more commercial offerings on the market. Ethnic parades, a pair of television networks, and countless new radio programs, magazines, and websites are catapulting Latin culture into the American consciousness on a daily basis. I hope you find ¡Cocinando! a tasty addition to this continuing success story.

MAMBO MANIA

POPULAR DANCE MUSIC

1940s–1960s

During the 1940s and 1950s, independent labels that catered specifically to Latino audiences tended to feature stiff portraits of musicians or colorful illustrations that condescendingly harped on the perceived primitive nature of the music. Though they may have cheapened the product, in retrospect we can be thankful for the window into the past these covers now provide.

Debonair Cuban heartthrob Desi Arnaz embodied the Hollywood ideal of the Latin Lover: light-skinned enough to be non-threatening to white American womanhood, but good enough at covering darker-skinned Miguelito Valdés' hit "Babalú" to be convincing on stage. On the cover of this 78 RPM record of the song, a "primitive" font zig-zags across a black field as Desi stands improbably freeze-framed in the midst of a drum solo. More exotic is *Voice of the Xtabay,* in which the "Peruvian Princess of the 20 Octaves," one Yma Sumac (Amy Camus backwards, anyone?), strikes a dramatic Technicolor pose while a savage stone idol menaces her from on high. Dynamic layout and bold colors save this from the heap of laughable "lounge" covers so in vogue in the 1990s.

The starkly affecting *Pachanga con Puente* shows percussionist extaordinaire Tito Puente heralding a would-be dance craze (the *pachanga*) with his futuristic *echotone*, the first fiberglass conga. Joe Cuba was particularly pleased with the adjacent cover, an Embajador Records bootleg that shows him with his trend-setting, homemade conga rack which, with the ingenious help of some household plumbing, allowed the *conguero* the freedom and visibility afforded by playing in a standing position.

In the early days, Latin independents used an arsenal of graphic (often racist) caricatures and nostalgic folk references to poke fun at Latinos in a naive yet visually arresting way. (See the depiction of the blind Afro-Cuban composer Arsenio Rodriguez on his album *Sabroso y caliente.*) There were also plenty of cheesy deluxe photos, such as the one used on the exploitative Charlie Palmieri bootleg, *Lo Ultimo.* Meanwhile, major labels that featured Latin music, notably RCA and Capitol, switched from the cartoon illustration-style used on albums for Beny Moré and bandleader Xavier Cugat to the modern "glamour" photographic shots that swept the advertising world in the 1950s. *Havana, 3 a.m.* epitomizes this approach. While conveying received notions of Latin primitivism, flamboyance, drama, and sensuality, it effectively sets a mood and assures the prospective buyer that a spicy, taboo-breaking evening is in the offing. *Watermelon Man!*, featuring the eponymous crossover hit penned by Herbie Hancock and made famous by Mongo Santamaría, was a precursor to the heady combo of soul and Latin that became "boogaloo" in the late 1960s. The intimate portrait of the glamorous white cover girl is pure Madison Avenue swank, the title racist kitsch, but somehow this juxtaposition manages to convey the thoroughly modern mix within.

Izzy Sanabria burst into this naive, patronizing, and tacky design world like a cleansing flood. His desire was to banish the generic spot illustration covers (see the billboardlike *Discoteca Latina*) and boxing-style dance posters that were the norm. As a child, Sanabria was always copying product labels in his mother's kitchen and putting on plays with boyhood friend and fellow artist and designer Waler Velez. After a stint in the army and as a professional dancer in barrio-area clubs, Sanabria worked in the advertising world, honing his skills as a packager.

His first cover, *Pacheco y su Charanga con Elliot Romero*, designed in 1961, was for Al Santiago's fledgling Bronx label Alegre. Bold in orange and black, that seminal cover elevated the level of artistry in Latin record design. Here, Pacheco's silhouette brings to mind an African sculpture in ebony. Sanabria consciously chose to use fine art over photography, driven by his belief that a crafted symbolic representation of the bandleader would stand out more than a photograph: "The album cover was like a woodcut of Pacheco, and it captures him perfectly in all his skinny, energetic essence. To this day, he wears that image made in gold, around his neck.... The little imperfections and extra lines in it gave the whole thing an electrical movement, which is the way he moved on stage."

Other assignments for Alegre followed, including *The Alegre All-Stars Vol. 3: "Lost & Found,"* which featured an unprecedented full-cover comic strip story starring Latin musicians. The narrative, about a missing tape, was "a goof," according to Sanabria, but was ingenious in that it demanded that the buyer acquire the other volumes from the series to resolve the story.

Another young and multi-talented designer followed soon after, helping to raise the stakes in Latin album aesthetics. Ely Besalel, originally from Colombia but raised in Brooklyn, trained himself to draw figures on the long subway rides to school, ultimately studying graphic design in college. He owed his start to a lot of hard work and a little luck: "I was a waiter in the Catskill resorts as a teenager. One night I was hitching a ride and a station wagon comes by just filled with Latino guys and instruments. It was Joe Cuba. We drove around a bit, had a laugh, then they dropped me off and Cuba said 'Listen man, every night after we play the Pines, we go jam at Grossinger's. Other musicians fall by, it's a gas.' Some years after the Catskills incident, when I was showing my work at [the record label] Roulette, Joe Cuba walks in and yells 'You!' He remembered me! That's how I got to do work for his label, Tico." Commissions for stalwarts like Celia Cruz, Jimmy Sabater, and Tito Puente followed. For these artists, Besalel provided a unique vision that had the comfort of familiarity but also something of an outsider feel—*Cuban Dance Festival* is a vibrant example of his artistic sensibility. "I never accepted things at face value, I never 'designed down,'" says Besalel. "I liked to experiment. I never lived in el Barrio, and I didn't feel obligated to buy [the prevailing Latin aesthetics of the day], or to crossover into the mainstream either. I was unencumbered by those expectations.

RhuMBa
with
CARLOS
MOLINA
and his Music of the Americas
Booth
Capitol
RECORDS

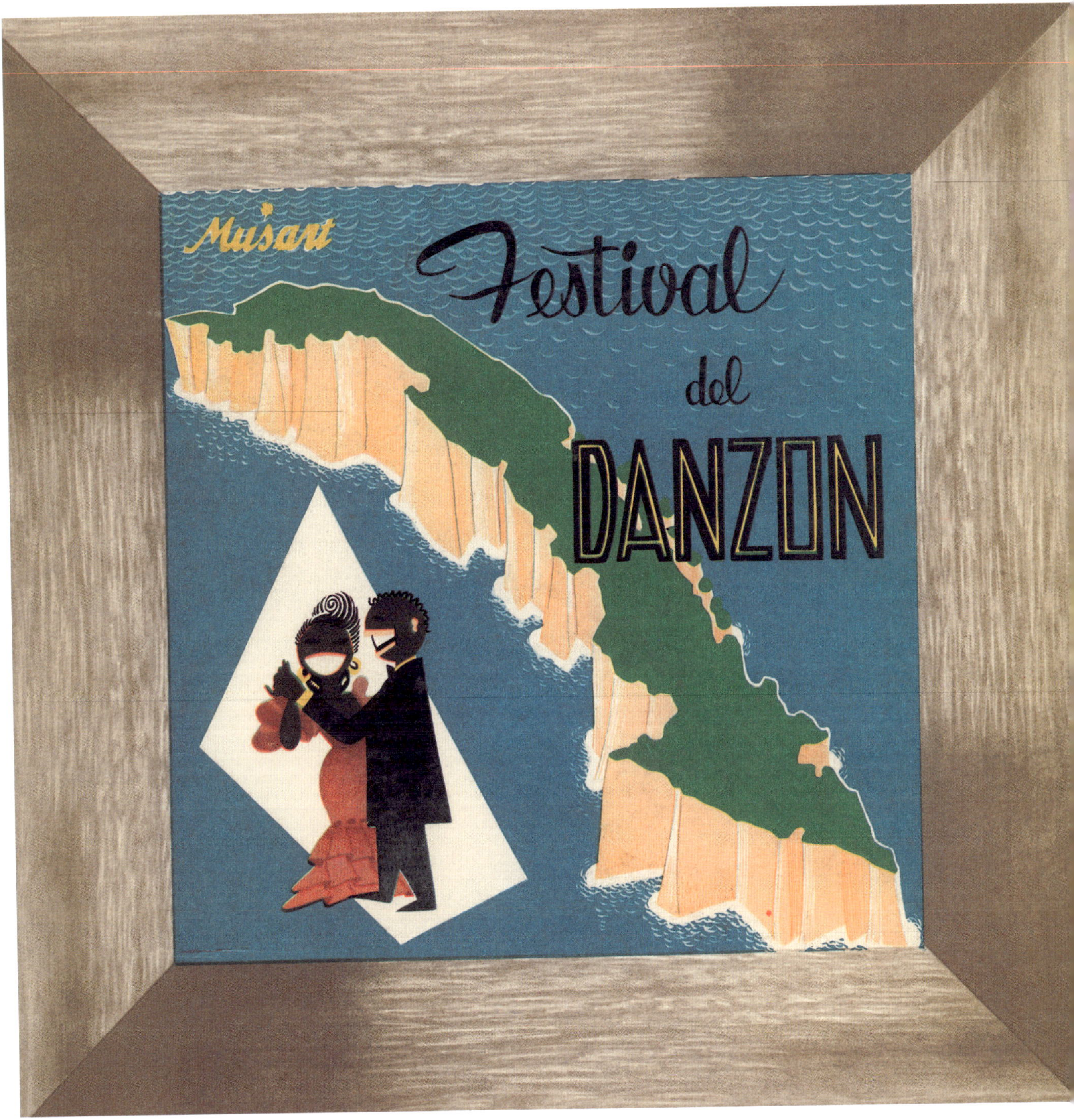
Musart
Festival
del
DANZON

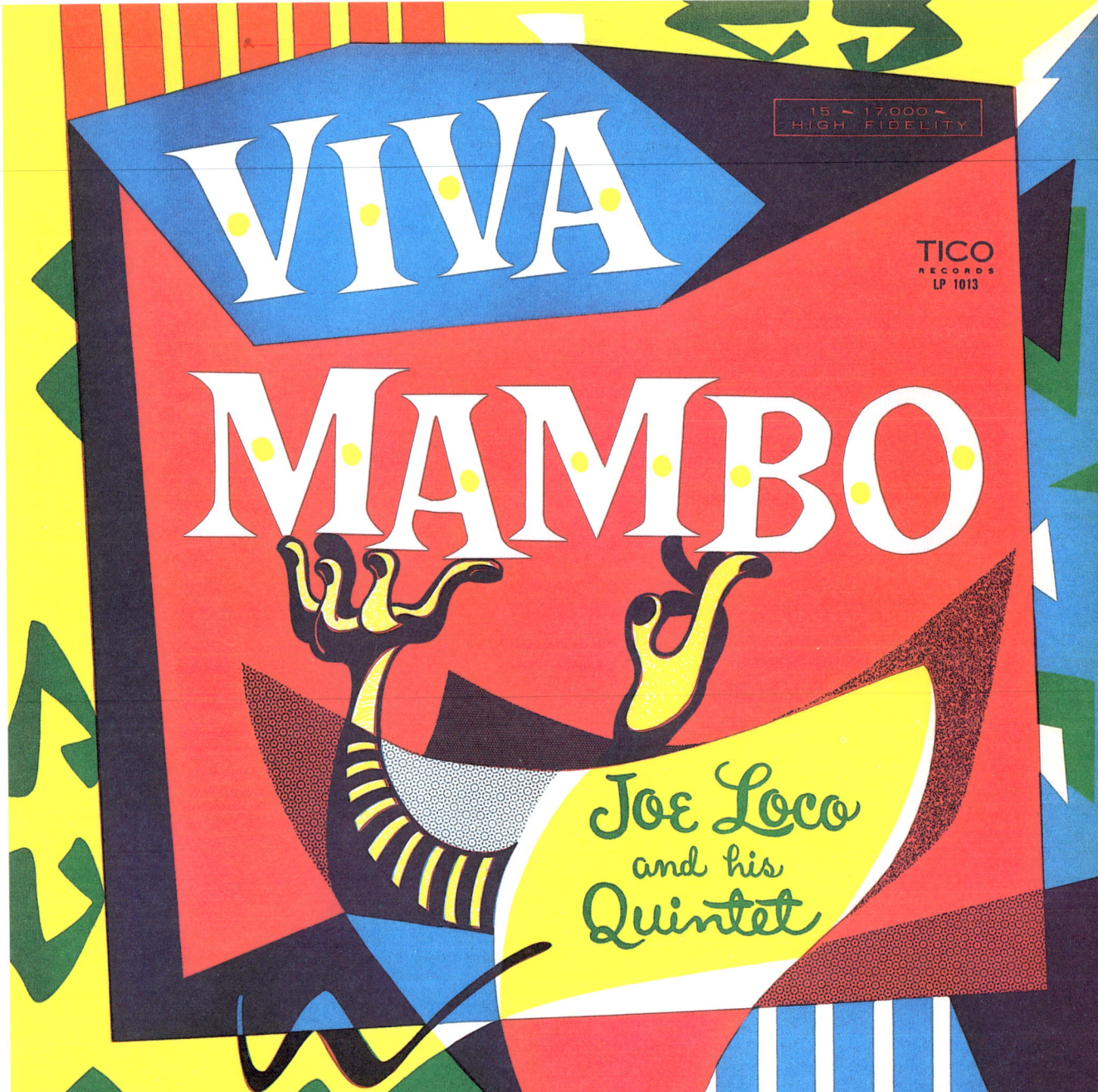

6006
EL GLOBO RECORDS
DISCOTECA LATINA
PRESENTA
Tito Puente
TITO RODRIGUEZ
Joe Loco
Machito
Alfredito
Martino Savanto

ARSENIO RODRÍGUEZ Y SU CONJUNTO

ANTILLA
MLP-586

SABROSO Y CALIENTE

- BUENAVISTA EN GUAGUANCO
- LA FONDA DE BIENVENIDO
- RECUERDO BIEN
- CARRAGUAO ALANTE
- HAY FUEGO EN EL 23
- MAMI ME GUSTO
- QUE FELIZ YO FUERA
- BESAME AQUI
- BLANCA PALOMA
- DEVUELVEME LA ILUSION
- ADORENLA COMO A MARTI

Havana, 3 a.m.

RCA VICTOR
LPM-1257
A "New Orthophonic" High Fidelity Recording

Perez Prado
and his orchestra

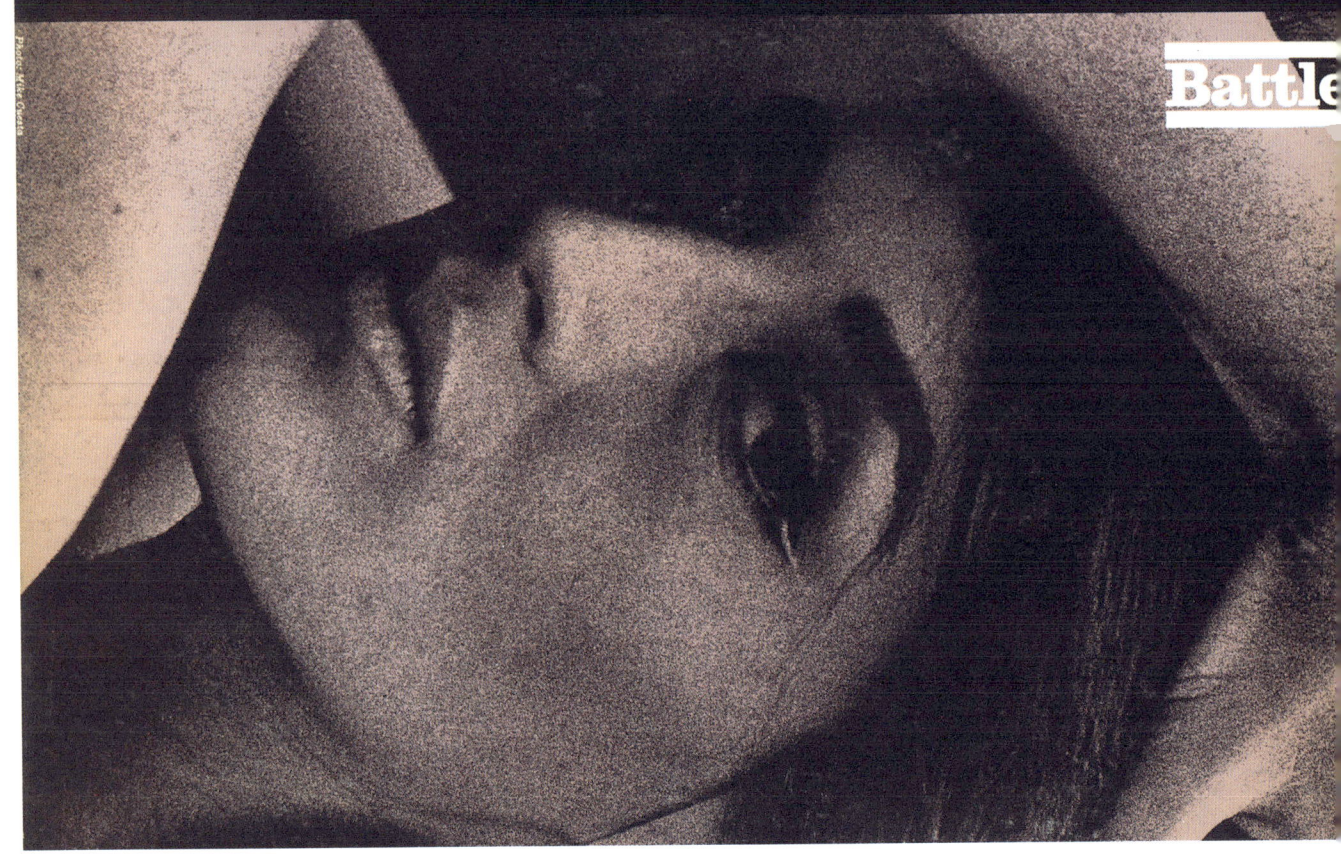

Hi-Fi

Pacheco y su Charanga

CON ELLIOT ROMERO

Juan Carlos Copes AND MARIA NIEVES

INTRODUCING

LA MILONGA

WITH ENRIQUE MENDEZ AND HIS ARGENTINIAN ORQUESTRA

Patty 102

MACHITO & HIS ORCHESTRA

SI=SI, NO=NO

LP 1033

TICO
HIGH FIDELITY

A DIVISION OF ROULETTE RECORDS INC.

DESIGN: ROBERT BROWNJOHN / BROWNJOHN, CHERMAYEFF & GEISMAR

STEREO
RS 809 SD

Command records

BONGOS BONGOS BONGOS

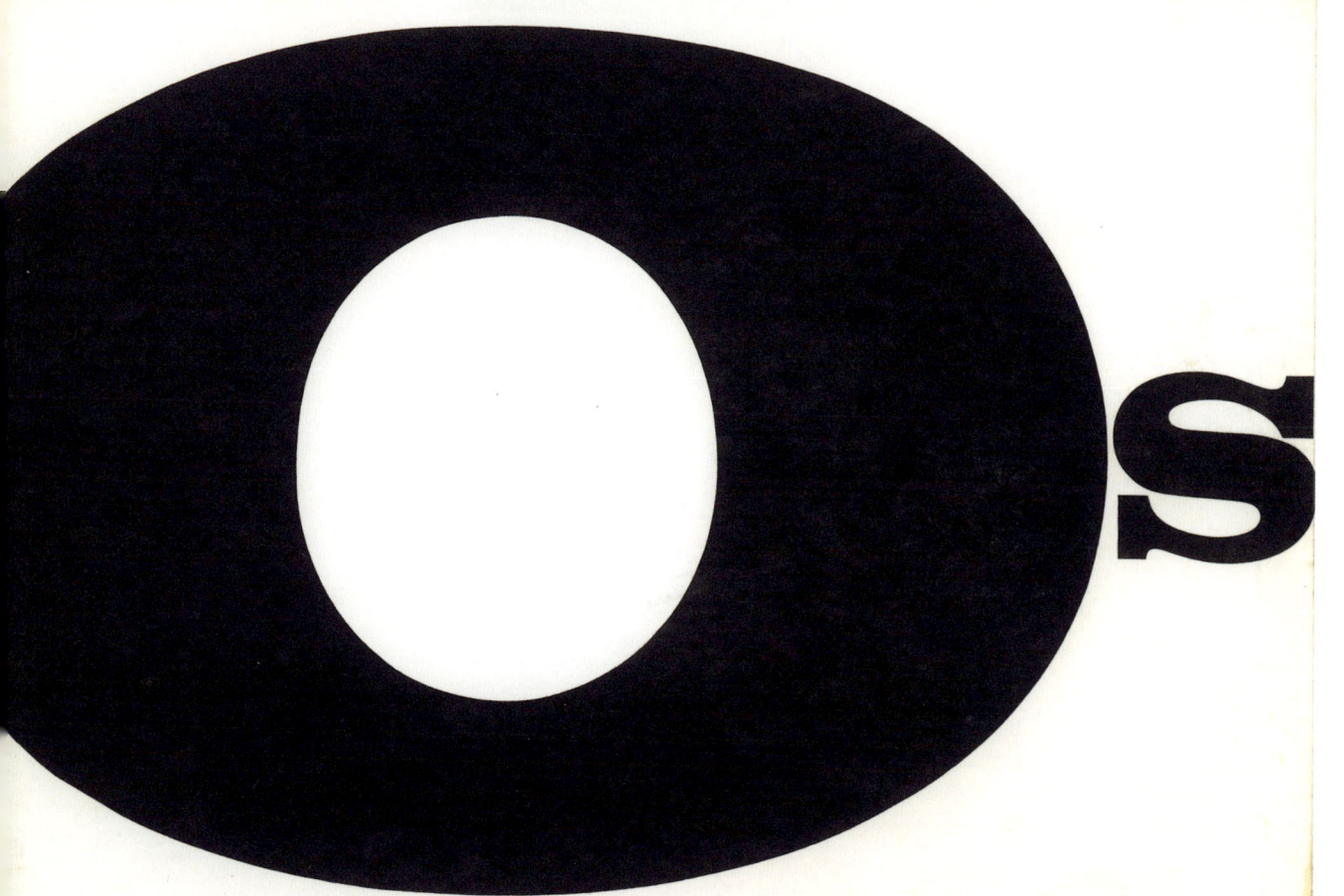

BONGOS BONGOS BONGOS

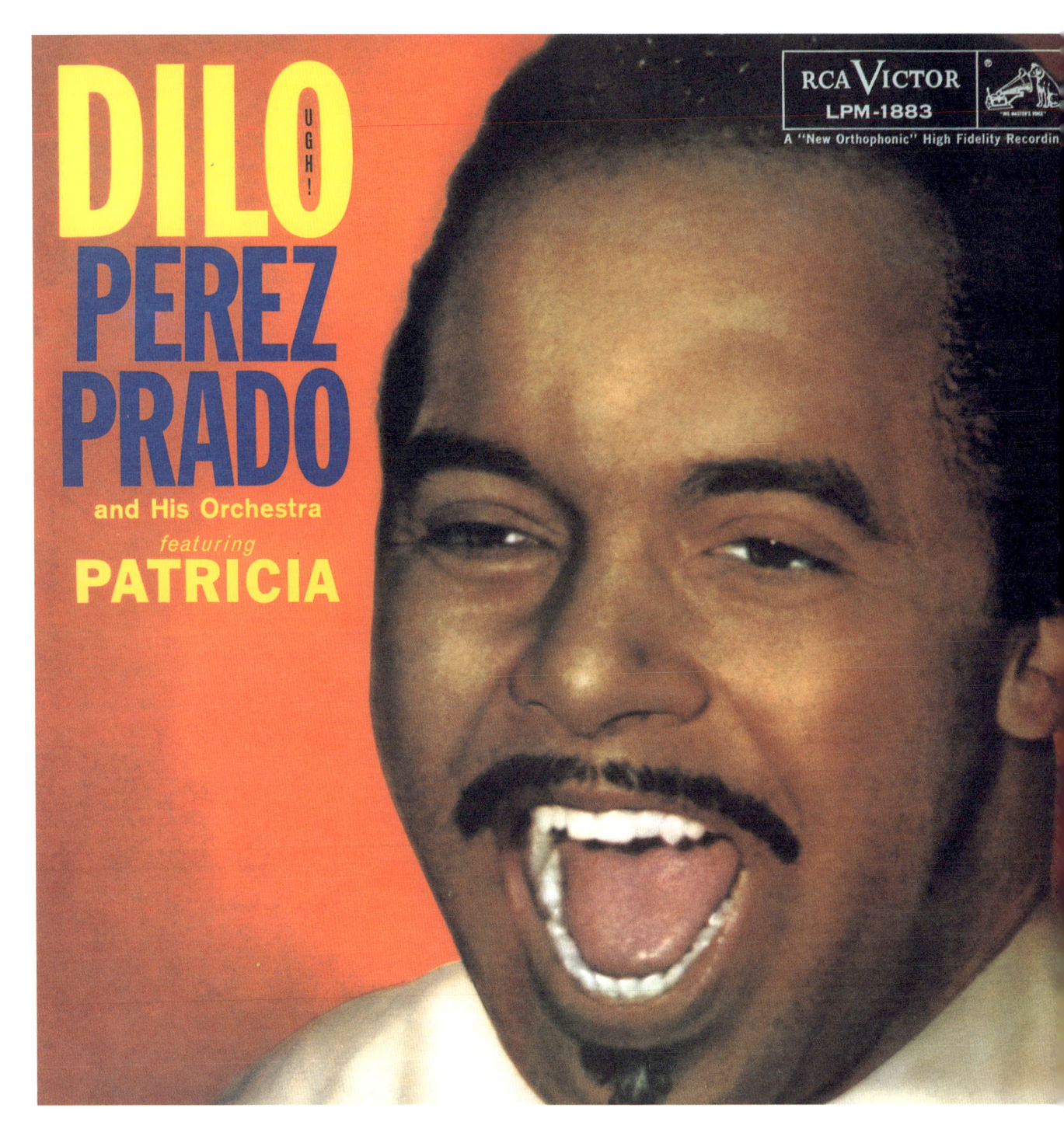

DILO UGH!
PEREZ PRADO
and His Orchestra
featuring
PATRICIA

RCA VICTOR
LPM-1883
A "New Orthophonic" High Fidelity Recording

maype
Musicalidad
en SEPIA
Cuní
CON
Chappotín
Y SUS
ESTRELLAS

CUBOP

LATIN JAZZ

1940s–PRESENT

> Machito's LP [*Afro-Cuban Jazz*] was one of those documents that changed my life. I made my fellow roommates at Yale listen to it in 1951. We marveled at everything, even the cover.
> —Robert Farris Thompson

Jazz and dance music parted ways after World War II, but it was at the nexus of the two genres that Cubop, that frenetic child of mambo, was formed. Machito's *Afro-Cuban Jazz*, with its deceptively simple cover designed by David Stone Martin, set the tone for the genre, with a declamatory pair of biracial arms raised in ritual ecstasy set against a blood red background of dynamic soundwaves, the perfect metaphor for the profound fusion at the heart of Latin jazz. Martin's intense linear aesthetic was soon adopted by other designers, as illustrated by the stark rendering and dynamic cropping on albums for Pete Terrace, Sabu Martinez, and the Cal Tjader Quintet. In fact, over a ten year stretch beginning in 1954, Tjader had the most visually engaging string of albums of any Latin musician. As the historian Robert Farris Thompson has noted, "Tjader's album covers were a jump ahead in terms of artistic quality, consistently better than anything... ever seen in Latin jazz. In those days the liner notes were the only literature we had to learn about the music and who was creating it, and Cal's were fantastic. They were more than just records, they were like cultural guides."

Back in 1953, Tjader, a vibist, along with bassist Al McKibbon and pianist George Shearing, heard Tito Puente and Machito at the Palladium and were thus inspired to incorporate Latin rhythms and melodies into their arrangements. Shearing's *Latin Escapade* sold fifty-thousand copies, an unprecedented number for Latin jazz at the time. The deluxe cover shot romanticizes that Palladium encounter, conjuring the enticing demimonde of an exotic beatnik bar complete with entwined couple, red wine, and an invitingly seductive mambo dancer. The florid *Mambo with Cal Tjader's Quintet* riffs on stereotypes of strutting Hispanic masculinity. It also highlights the crucial role that Afro-Cuban culture played during the post-Swing era in reuniting jazz with its so-called "jungle" roots, helping nurture the seeds of a rising African consciousness in the U.S. black community.

While jazz opened itself to free structures and abstraction in the 1960s, Latin jazz kept its feet firmly planted on the ground. The mellifluously titled *Cándido in Indigo* is the first of many instances in which the ace Cuban percussionist shows off his powerful physique and radically shaved head, this time bathed in a jazzy blue light (percussionists seem to generate the most dramatic cover art). *Puente in Percussion* aptly brings together the two main elements that construct Nuyorican identity: ancestral roots symbolized by the conga drums, and the driving jackhammer rhythms of the modern metropolis. Reflecting his label's crossover ambitions, Mongo Santamaría's groovy *Mongo '70* displays a classic Age of Aquarius backdrop, though the *conguero* himself shows his allegiance to his roots, resplendent in African hat, tunic, and beads.

Moving into the 1970s, Latin jazz covers mirrored the general trends in jazz fusion: a predilection for complex narrative or surreal imagery, often fitting in with the values and aesthetics of the non-Latin-owned labels that put them out. Chicano jazz trumpeter and former Santana and El Malo sideman Luis Gasca's outrageous 1976 *Collage* cover is a trippy, tour-de-force portrait by artist Jamie Putnam, bringing to mind both pop art and the world of high fashion.

While many Latin jazz covers of the 1980s and 1990s featured uninspired photos of live performances or flat digital graphics, there were some with creative art that hearkened back to earlier styles or had something to say about the unique fusion of the "Latin Tinge." For a set of Castro-era recordings called *Forbidden Cuba in the 80's*, released in 1998 by RMM Records, art director Carlo Moralishvili and this author used images of contemporary Latinos by Miami-based Cuban photographer Jorge Garcia Torres. A conga and cigar logo coupled with a tobacco-leaf header, color-coded for each decade, helped tie the series together.

World Pacific's own Castro-era series, *The Music of Cuba*, was the first of its kind. *El jazz cubano* actually utilizes a painting depicting flamenco artists in Málaga, Spain. Continuing that bright, festive feeling, Cuban-born muralist and painter Viredo Espinosa's 1997 acrylic *The Cabildo Is Coming* graces Poncho Sanchez's Picante release, *Afro-Cuban Fantasy*. Viredo spent years attending Afro-Cuban rituals and celebrations in his home town of Regla, a colonial port across the bay from Havana with rich religious traditions (a *cabildo* is a social/religious association formed originally by and for Cuban blacks born in Africa). Though the stylized renderings for *El jazz cubano* and the Sanchez CD may seem folksy, they were made by artists who know and appreciate the music intimately.

This chapter ends with a design inspired by the cigar box, one of the most venerable Latin design paradigms. Cuban saxophonist Paquito D'Rivera's take on the seminal *descarga* jam sessions of Israel "Cachao" Lopez in the 1950s is skillfully represented by gold foil and cigar-band shapes—a harbinger of the nostalgic look that would take over the industry with the coming of the Buena Vista Social Club.

MG C-689

MACHITO
AFRO-CUBAN JAZZ

The Music of Chico O'Farrill

SUPERVISED BY NORMAN GRANZ

muenster-dummel
HI-FI
recording

CLEF RECORDS

GNPD 23
GENE NORMAN PRESENTS
DIZZY GILLESPIE
and his big band
IN CONCERT
FEATURING
CHANO POZO
WINNER
GRAND PRIX
AWARD
JAZZ HOT
MAGAZINE
PARIS, FRANCE
J. BRANDT

Fantasy 3232
HIGH FIDELITY

CAL TJADER QUINTET

Sabu's Jazz Espagnole

ALEGRE

ISRAEL SANABRIA

MAMBO JAZZ

TICO RECORDS
15 ~ 17,000 ~
HIGH FIDELITY
LP 1028

pete terrace
& his Latin Jazz Quintet

THE NEARNESS OF YOU

LEE-MYLES ASSOC., N.Y.C.

THE GEORGE SHEARING QUINTET

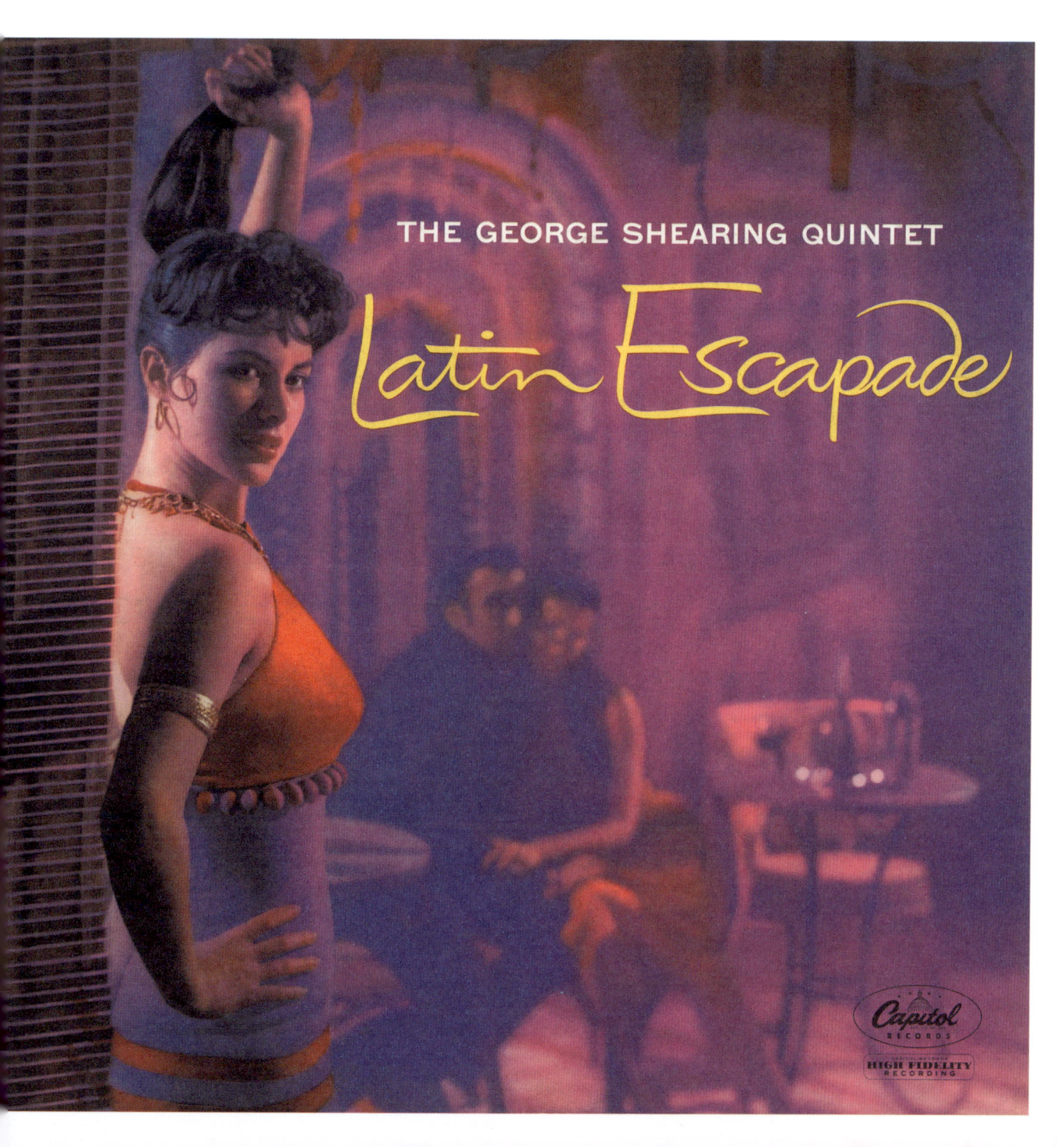

Latin Escapade

Capitol RECORDS
HIGH FIDELITY RECORDING

Mambo! with Tjader

Cal Tjader Quintet

fantasy 3326
HIGH FIDELITY

CANDIDO in indigo

A STEREOPHONIC RECORD

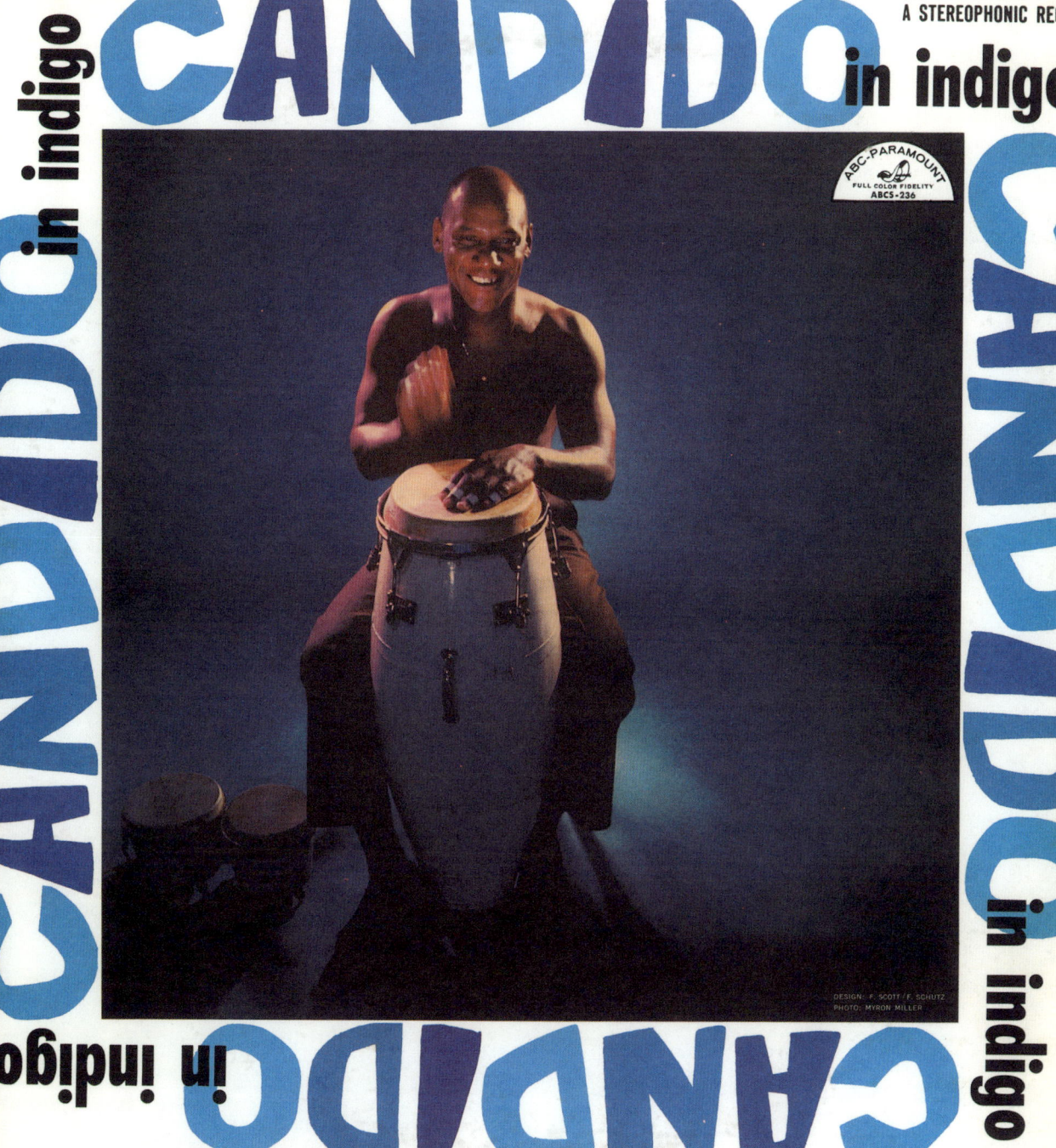

ABC-PARAMOUNT
FULL COLOR FIDELITY
ABCS-236

DESIGN: F. SCOTT / F. SCHUTZ
PHOTO: MYRON MILLER

CUBAN JAM SESSIONS IN MINIATURE
"DESCARGAS"

CACHAO y su Ritmo Caliente

Puente in Percussion

LP-1011
TICO

Mongo '70

STEREO
SD 1567

ATLANTIC

LUIS GASCA
COLLAGE

F-9504

Fantasy

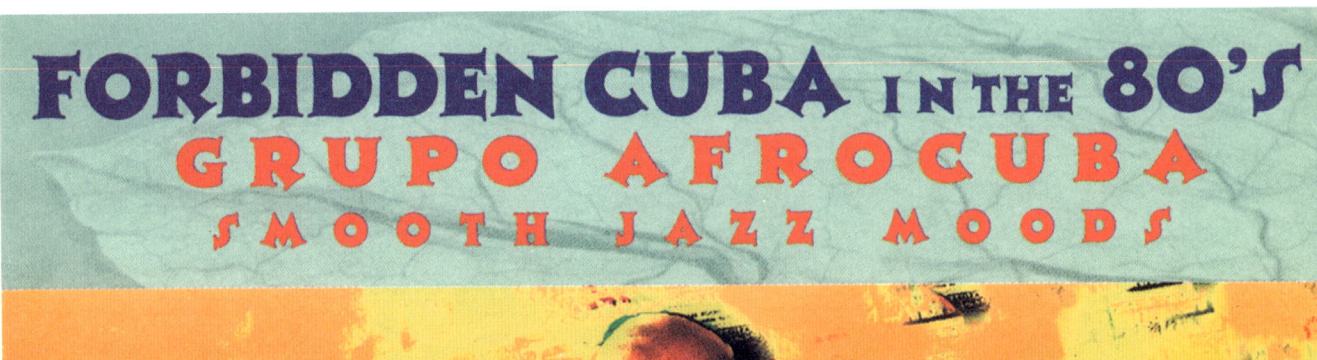

FORBIDDEN CUBA IN THE 80'S
GRUPO AFROCUBA
SMOOTH JAZZ MOODS

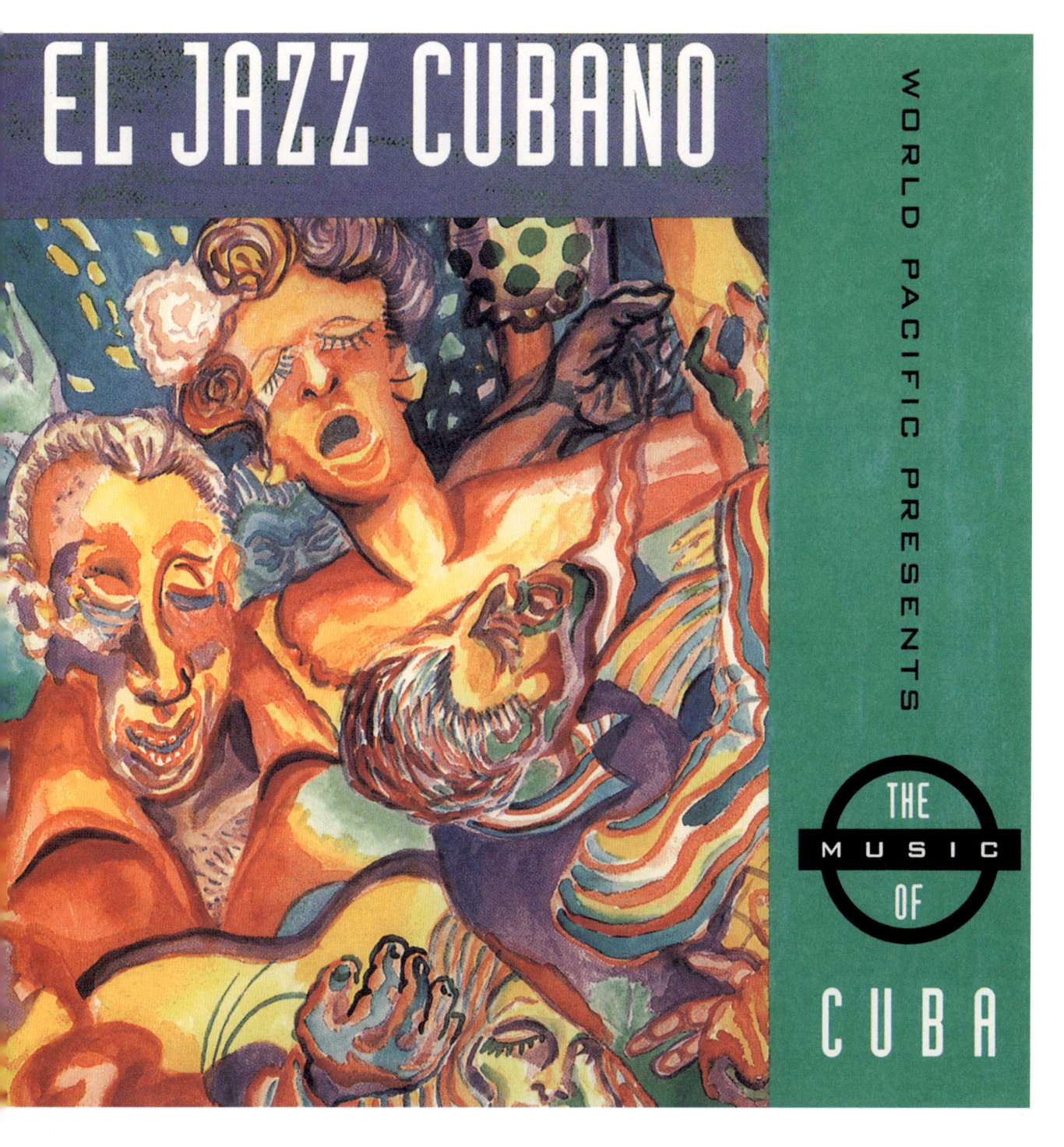

EL JAZZ CUBANO

WORLD PACIFIC PRESENTS

THE MUSIC OF CUBA

PONCHO SANCHEZ

Afro-Cuban Fantasy

PAQUITO D'RIVERA PRESENTS

JOSÉ »CHOMBO« SILVA
JUANITO MÁRQUEZ · ISRAEL
»CACHAO« LÓPEZ · ANDY GARCIA
JESÚS CAUNEDO · WALDEMAR
GÓMEZ · ARMANDITO ROMEU
LEOPOLDO »PUCHO« ESCALANTE
HORACIO »EL NEGRO« HERNÁNDEZ
ALFREDO PÉREZ · TATA PALAU
CARLOS GÓMEZ

PAQUITO D' RIVERA
NICKY ORTA · ALFREDO
»CHOCOLATE« ARMENTEROS
ROGELIO »YEYITO« RIVERO
JUAN PABLO TORRES · RIGO
HERRERA · VICTOR VALDÉS
RENÉ TOLEDO · MIKE ORTA
ENRIQUE »KIKE« HERNÁNDEZ
EDITO MARTINEZ

40 YEARS OF CUBAN JAM SESSION

PREFACE BY
GUILLERMO CABRERA INFANTE

ORIZA

FOLKLORIC, *TÍPICO*, AND RELIGIOUS MUSIC

1950s–PRESENT

The vibrancy of Latin music springs from its vigorous root system. Whether the listener labels it folklore, *típico*, religious music, or music of the people, there is no denying that the traditional wellspring of the music is a living, changing, temporal force that is never stagnant. With that understood, this chapter does not concern itself solely with relics of the mid-twentieth century, but spans the entire time period covered in the book. Nor does it present Latin identities as fixed in a vacuum as part of a tradition devoid of contemporary inspiration. Silvestre Mendez's seminal *Oriza*, purportedly an album of folkloric and religious-based Afro-Cuban rhythms and chants, was actually a profoundly innovative modern hybrid. His unprecedented combination of multiple congas with swinging jazz transpositions of liturgical music effortlessly straddled the traditional and the popular worlds. The album's expressionistic cover painting, with its burning red background, seems to declare the power of the music, while Mendez's wide-open mouth proclaims his arrival on the scene and heralds his exposure of the previously sacrosanct and occult world of Afro-Atlantic music.

It has been said that Mongo Santamaría was reticent to mix the sacred and the profane in his music, but he had no problem adapting his friend Silvestre's five-conga attack to his own sound. In the 1950s the two collaborated on the historic *Drums and Chants*, represented here in its reissued form from the mid-1970s, with an initially jarring juxtaposition of tradition and innovation by artist Charlie Rosario. With this new jacket design, we see the move from exoticism to nativism, with Rosario consciously reveling in his African roots. Figures and landscape are purposefully stylized, simply cut from recycled fabric swatches, and the entire field is flattened—not to poke fun at folkways, but to call attention to the record's ties with tradition. A modern font and a halftone portrait of Mongo's face (collaged from newsprint media) convey a sense of contemporary style. "I wanted the primitive look but I wanted the execution to be modern," said Rosario. The other Santamaría "traditional" album presented here, the rare *Afro-Cuban Drums*, has a futuristic look more in keeping with a modern jazz LP than a traditional field recording.

Many other covers employ an apparent lack of representational sophistication to convey complex attitudes about race, identity, and tradition. In the case of Celina and Reutilio González and Gina Martin's *Fiesta Santera*, there is a form of reverse racism no doubt engendered by a marketing campaign preoccupied with ideas of authenticity and agency. While the music industry's prayers may have been answered in the 1950s by Latin music's Elvis figures, Desi Arnaz and Tito Rodriguez (white men who could "sing black"), Suaritos Records no doubt employed this pseudo-minstrel portrait of the black *santera* and drummers as a ploy to hide the fact that the three performers were in fact white *guajiros* (Cuban *jíbaros*) playing "country" music. Ironically, these interpreters of *santería* material were actually practitioners of that Afro-Atlantic diaspora religion and held no real racist prejudices of their own.

Fiesta Santera: Toques y Cantos Santero Lucumí is another album that is not what it seems: a recording of African-derived sacred music disguised as a collection of Catholic liturgies. Though the cover sports a clumsily collaged display of Christian saints and seems through its "inept" presentation to be a budget knock-off of some kind, it was in fact a notably influential recording made with serious intent and conviction, one of the few authentic examples of the genre available in the 1960s. The layout imitates the crowded shelf displays of candles and figurines typical of the *botánicas* (religious goods stores) commonly found in Latin neighborhoods, where the album was intended for sale.

The norm for 1950s and 1960s folkloric *típico* music might best be represented by the artless but authentic *Guaguanco Afro-Cubano* and the downright bawdy/gaudy *El plenero* (that the record label, Ninfa, literally means "nymph" but is slang for "chick," says it all). Nuyorican artist Manny Vega's masterful painting for *Puerto Rico Puerto Rico Mi Tierra Natal* is a fascinating portrait of the dual traditions of African (*bomba, plena*) and European (*jíbaro*) roots that co-exist on that island but, as Morton Marks writes in the liner notes, "each reflects its own geographic, historical, and cultural development." He adds, in reference to the lyrics, but just as easily applicable to the artwork: "Behind the poignant image...lies a set of powerful connections that bind Puerto Ricans to each other and to a shared heritage and homeland. Whether we call it folk or traditional, the emotional intensity... arises from the special feelings and experiences intimately known only to members of a tightly knit community." Although the dark-skinned *pleneros* and lighter *jíbaritos* depicted on the cover may be bisected by a median line that splits night and day, they do share the same space and are unified by the bold palate and rendering.

An influx of *santería* themes worked their way into late 1960s and early 1970s salsa. Ely Besalel's cover for La Lupe's *La Reina: The Queen* on Tico might be the first instance of a non-folkloric recording that puts Afro-Cuban spiritual identity up front for all to see. Warren Flagler's photograph finds La Lupe dressed in the traditional white colonial dress of the *yawó* initiate, with copper bracelets, *santería collar* necklaces, and head modestly covered in a traditional wrap. But there is something wrong with this picture—that pose is anything but pure. La Lupe may be in the act of prostration before the gods, but she is looking up at the viewer with impish insouciance, her long disheveled hair curling out from under the wrap. It is clear that crazy laugh of hers is in there somewhere, bubbling; that at any moment she may yell "Ay, yi, yi, yi ahí na má, baby!" and whip out her breast the way she did on stage. Besalel's layout recalls the Tijuana Brass whipped cream cover (a monstrosity that surpasses most Latin deluxe styles), though Besalel says that he had not seen it at the time. Certainly, it comes from an entirely different intellectual place.

Mongo Santamaría's 1972 Atlantic release, *Up from the Roots*, is groundbreaking in that it is a concerted effort to take the listener on an evolutionary journey—a folkloric concept album—traveling from elemental solo-voice singing in African tongue through various traditional forms and ending with the latest in contemporary Latin music, all helpfully delineated in the credits. The cover's seemingly simple design was the product of a tortuous and dishonest process, but it ultimately resulted in one of the most successful Latin covers of the period. First, Charlie Rosario provided a series of designs featuring a primordial figure playing a drum. This set the tone for the album, though the image was rejected and Rosario dumped. (He did, however, recycle the image for the *Kako* album, that appears in the Salsita chapter.) The label then brought in Sanabria, whose design included a primitive mask run full-bleed with bold type across the eyes. "Next thing I know it comes out with my basic design but a different mask. I was pissed! I went to Atlantic and complained," said Sanabria. The final image, taken by house designer Richard Mantell from a West African monument created around 200 A.D., makes a direct link to the ancestral roots of the music, in effect singing the same song that starts the album.

Daniel Ponce's debut, *New York Now!*, rounds out this section. The power of its striking cover is augmented by recent events beyond the scope of the record's music. The title and montage art encapsulate perfectly what the music incorporates into the album's heady grooves, a mix of ancient and new summed up in the composition "Africa contemporanea." Looming here in the background behind the New York cityscape is a paleolithic warrior face—an engaging metaphor for the persistence of folkways and the power of resistance that Latin roots-consciousness represents in the city.

ORIZA

AFRO-CUBAN RHYTHMS

SILVESTRE, El Rey del Canto Afro Cubano y Su Orquesta

MONGO SANTAMARIA
DRUMS AND CHANTS

VAYA
VAYA RECORDS JMVS 56
SERIES 0698
COMPATIBLE STEREO

ALP 1237

Ramito

EL CANTOR DE LA MONTAÑA

Ansonia

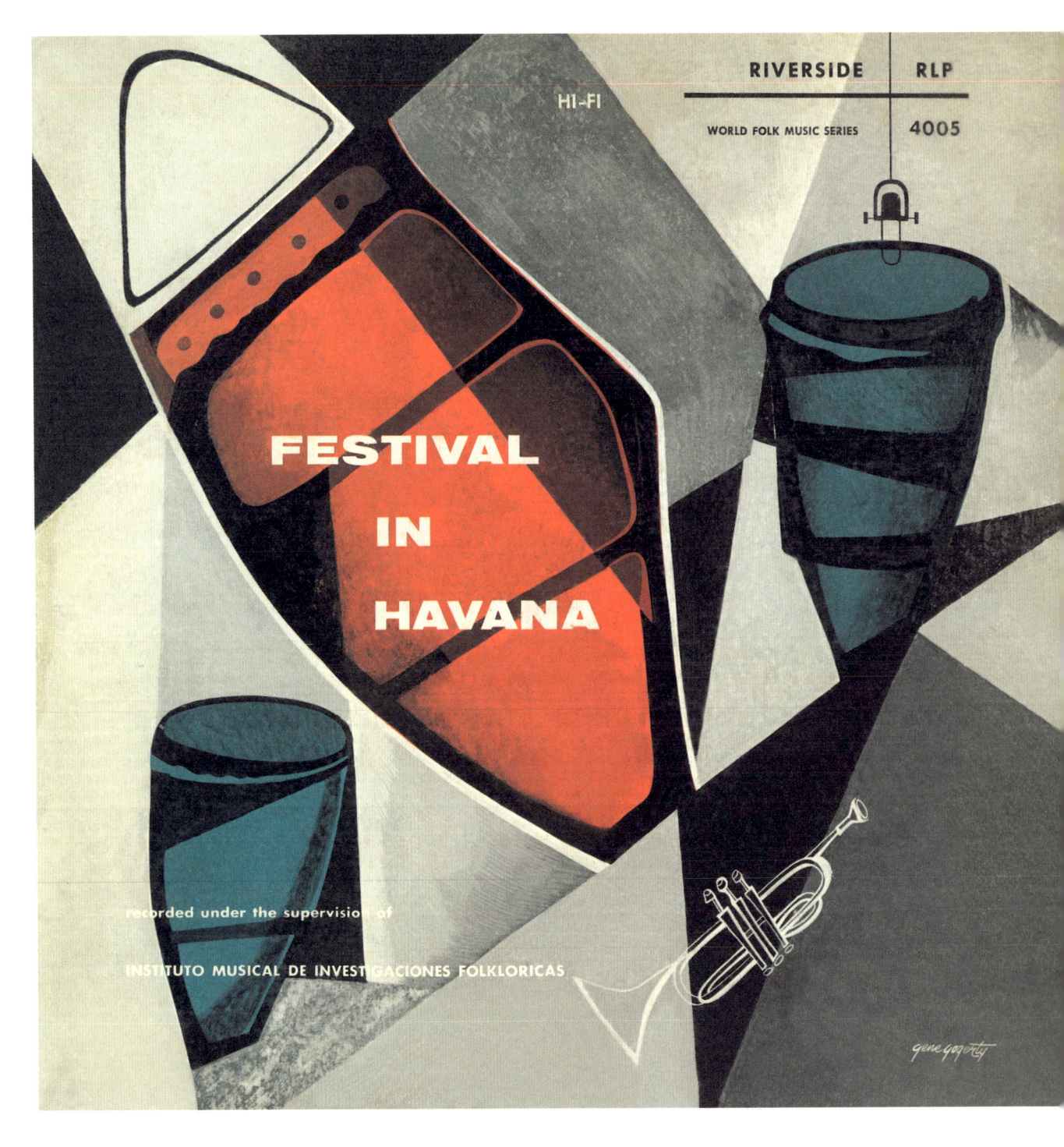

RIVERSIDE | RLP
HI-FI
WORLD FOLK MUSIC SERIES | 4005

FESTIVAL IN HAVANA

recorded under the supervision of

INSTITUTO MUSICAL DE INVESTIGACIONES FOLKLORICAS

gene goforty

SMC
Pro-Arte
LP592
HI FIDELITY

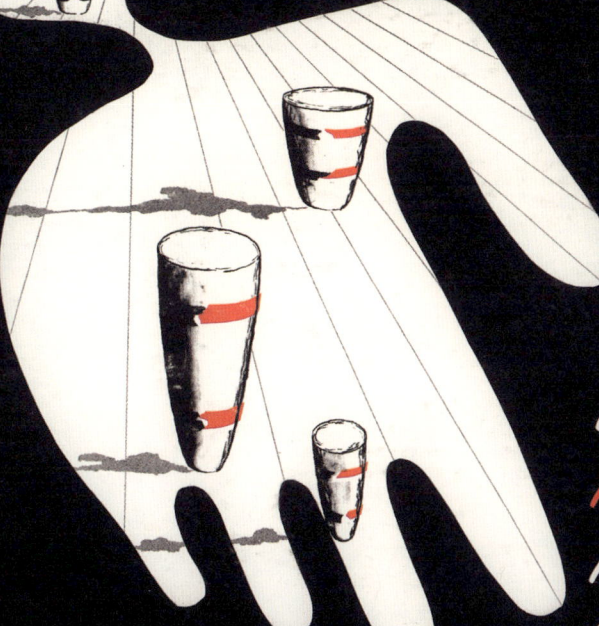

Mongo Santamaria's
AFRO-CUBAN DRUMS

with
Mercedita Valdes,
Monguito,
Chonguito,
Willy & Candito

FIESTA
SANTERA
SUARITOS
S-110
CELINA - REUTILIO
Y GINA MARTIN

FIESTA SANTERA

STEREO

SANTERO 375

TOQUES Y CANTOS SANTERO LUCUMI

GUAGUANCO AFRO - CUBANO

EL VIVE BIEN con el GRUPO FOLKLORICO de Alberto Zayas

Panart HIGH FIDELITY

EL PLENERO

JAIME DE JESUS
y su cuarteto 'Alma Alegre'

PUERTO RICO PUERTO RICO

LOS PLENEROS DE LA 21
CONJUNTO MELODIA TROPICAL
MI TIERRA NATAL

LA LUPE
ES LA REINA
LA LUPE
THE QUEEN
TICO
HIGH FIDELITY
DIVISION OF ROULETTE RECORDS INC.

EMILIO BARRETO PRESENTA

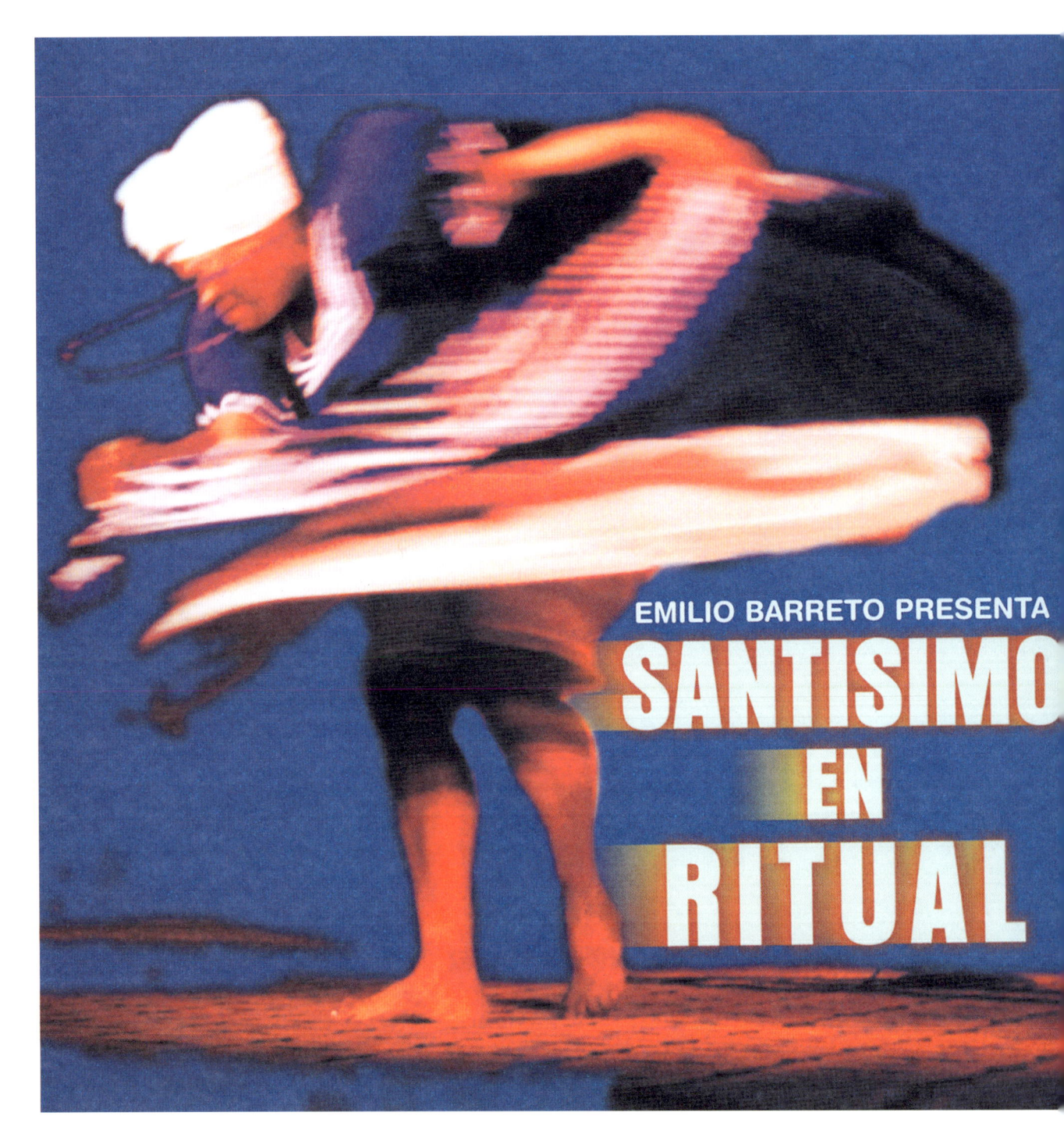

SANTISIMO EN RITUAL

TRIO LOS CONDES

ugando De Verdad	No Vendo El Corazón	Tú, La Noche y Yo	Mi Loca Fantasía	Fuiste Una Flor	Cuando Calienta El Sol
MI HADA	EL COFRE	PRECIOSA	NUNCA MAS	NO LO NIEGUES	TANTAS COSAS

Gema Records LPC-3032 STEREO

SABU
palo congo

BLP 156

THE FINEST IN JAZZ SINCE 1939
BLUE NOTE
A PRODUCT OF LIBERTY RECORDS

© LIBERTY RECORDS, INC

KUBANEY

MT 119 ALTA FIDELIDAD

RADIO PROGRESO

estampas de

Luis Carbonell

SALP 1477
STEREO
Ritmos y Cantos Callejeros
CORTIJO
Y
KAKO
y sus Tambores
Ansonia
RECORDS

Patato & Totico

LAT 10,006

Will play on both Mono and Stereo equipment.

Latino Series
MGM RECORDS

MONGO SANTAMARIA
UP FROM THE ROOTS

STEREO
ATLANTIC
SD 1621

DANIEL PONCE

CELL 5005

NEW YORK NOW!

OAO

VIVA SOUL

BOOGALOO, LATIN SOUL, AND POPULAR DANCE MUSIC 1960s

> Popular Latin bands...found themselves creating a musical common ground by introducing the trappings of Black American culture into their performances and thus getting the Black audiences involved and onto the dance floor. Boogaloo music in general was intended to constitute this meeting place between Puerto Ricans and Blacks, and by extension, between Latin music and the musical culture of the United States.
>
> —Juan Flores

The 1960s were a time of upheaval within the Latin music world, and with the advent of Latin Soul—known variously as shing-a-ling, *bugalú*, *jala-jala*, and just plain boogaloo—some of the older players of the previous decades had to make way for a new generation of upstarts. Visionary designers like Sanabria, Besalel, and John Murello helped the producers Al Santiago, George Goldner, Morris Levy, and Jerry Masucci capitalize on this new craze that was sweeping the clubs and street corners of New York's barrios. Covers were starting to openly reflect the changing attitudes toward sexuality and drugs, as evidenced by Orchestra Harlow's debut for Fania, *Heavy Smokin'*.

As the historian Juan Flores has noted, it was the song "Bang Bang" (by velvet-voiced Jimmy Sabater with the Joe Cuba Sextet), released first as a single and then on the album *Wanted Dead or Alive*, that put Latin Soul on the map. Following soon after was Cuba's *My Man Speedy!* (as in Speedy Gonzalez). While the titles on this album reference the counter-culture ("Psychedelic Baby"), the Sextet still looked like mods in their sharkskin suits and Caesar haircuts. "The cover was my idea," recounts Cuba, "you know, the guys bouncin' off my bongos! It's a happy picture.... We have to express our joy to get over problems. I was a big admirer of Xavier Cugat's showmanship.... I didn't want the dead stiff look that a lot of bands had."

New social freedoms were reflected in swirling and graffiti-based fonts, day-glo colors, and the emergence of the deluxe aesthetic (Johnny Zamot's *Tell It Like It Is* being a prime example). Charlie Rosario was just a young art student in 1968 when Charlie Palmieri found him waiting out in the cold on Delancey Street in New York City, trying to get into an after-hours club to see Tito Puente. Hopefully tucked under his arm was a San Francisco-style psychedelic portrait of Puente. Palmieri took Rosario upstairs, where Rosario presented his proposal for Puente's album *The King*—and then asked for a meager $75 from the thrilled musician.

Izzy Sanabria ingeniously incorporated a subway sign for Joe Bataan's second release, *Subway Joe*—a harbinger of Sanabria's penchant for using everyday items and found objects in his design. "I was influenced by R. Crumb, 'underground comix,' psychedelic rock posters by [Victor] Moscoso and [Rick] Griffin, pop art, industrial design," says Sanabria. Larry Harlow, who had the first Latin psychedelic stage show, sheds a little more light on the convolutions of the era: "In the 1960s I bought all my clothes in the Village. On *El Exigente*, I'm wearing that crazy jacket. That's an ultraviolet film stock that Marty Topp used, and Izzy did the lettering by hand. Marty was a friend of mine who was very psychedelic. The year was 1967. I was following a sound one day up in the Catskill Mountains; I followed this high pitched, drawn-out tone for hours through the woods and the swamps. I was stoned on LSD, and I wound up following this frequency to this little gingerbread house, and this girl came out, pitching hay, and then [photographer] Marty Topp stuck out his head and said 'Come on in and have a cup of coffee.' I went in and they had this piano where all the keys were painted different colors, and I found out I had been listening to Yusef Lateef playing the oboe or something weird like that! Marty mentioned he took pictures, and right there I said 'You wanna do an album for me?' and he did, as well as one for Joe Bataan, [*Subway Joe*] and Ray Barretto [*Acid*]."

While many boogaloo-era album covers have a dated, *Austin Powers*-feel (see the TNT Boys' *Sex Symbols*), the LeBron Brothers' soulful *I Believe* design would not look out of place among today's hip hop covers. The stark, bold typography of Besalel's first Eddie Palmieri cover, *Justicia*, offers a timeless cry for justice. "I posed him there so small in the corner, he's thinking, worrying, and the issue of justice is so big. We spent a lot of time just rapping, really interesting conversations when I was planning covers for him," says Besalel. In fact, the two had an intimate, intellectual liaison that lasted through two decades, and included covers for albums, in addition to *Justicia*, such as *Vamos Pa'l Monte*, *Superimposition*, and *Unfinished Masterpiece*.

Also concerned with social issues and awakened to the alternative lifestyles of the times was vibist Harvey Averne, whose 1970 *Brotherhood* LP was designed by Sanabria. "I didn't like being on the cover of my albums," he said recently. "I told Izzy I'm not posing for any more pictures, so he did this great collage, with the kids all over my face, and this wild big breast on my forehead, like a mother to the Brotherhood. We thought [Fania president Jerry] Masucci wouldn't go for it, but I guess it snuck by, and I'm glad it did."

Former Cal Tjader sideman Willie Bobo's *Spanish Grease* and Tjader's own *Soul Sauce* are very important 1960s icons in that they prominently feature traditional ethnic *comida criolla*, highlighting the central role that Latino cuisine plays in the culture's self-definition.

Despite the serious messages and protest songs finding their way into Latin Soul set lists, and the awakening ethnic pride that would lead to a backlash against English lyrics, young Latin musicians kept their raucous sense of fun firmly intact. Juxtaposed with the somber frustration expressed in Palmieri's *Justicia*, Orchestra Harlow's *Me and My Monkey* makes for a study in goofiness. An anecdote from Larry Harlow expands on just how goofy it really was: "I came up with the idea. We were standing on the floor, and I was trying to keep a straight face. I was naked, and my brother Andy was inside the costume roasting his cookies off. We had the thing for 24 hours; it was costing Jerry a fortune, but we still had another twenty hours left. I said, 'What are we gonna do with a monkey suit?' So we went up to see [DJ] Symphony Sid, who was stoned all the time, and we snuck in on our hands and knees, under the glass in front of the booth at the radio station. We jumped into the studio and almost gave him a coronary on the air; he skipped a record when we popped up!" Meanwhile, Sanabria's flair for the dramatic and uncluttered takes a turn for the tender with his treatment of Jimmy Sabater's groundbreaking LP *El hijo de Teresa/Teresa's Son*. Here Sabater holds his mother, to whom the album is dedicated, in a protective embrace. "I took photos of Jimmy's mother, then I painted him inside her womb, using earth tones because the earth is our original mother, with the stars in the background," says Sanabria.

We finish this chapter with a new genre of urban documentary realism that crept in on the heels of the psychedelic revelry. Contrast the sexist imagery of Willie Bobo's *Juicy* with the slice-of-life snapshot on *Uno dos tres*, showing the local, unglamorous image of a *bodega*, the social hub of the barrio.

Besalel's cover for *Tito Puente en el Puente* [Tito Puente on the Bridge] metaphorically bridges the gap between the two worlds of Latin and soul, the public performer and the fan, the insular barrio and the larger metropolis that surrounds it. "I suggested he take his new wife...up on the bridge [for the cover]," recalls Besalel, mentioning that the bridge is also a symbol of the bond forged between two lovers when they marry. "I did the stretched lettering by hand; they are running toward Manhattan, and Warren [Flagler] captured their moment of happiness with his wide-angle lens."

Orchestra HARLOW

FANIA RECORDS 331

HEAVY SMOKIN'

WANTED Dead or Alive

The Joe Cuba Sextet

BANG! BANG! PUSH, PUSH, PUSH.

SE BUSCA Muerto o Vivo

El Sexteto de Joe Cuba

BANG! BANG! PUSH, PUSH, PUSH.

TICO HIGH FIDELITY
A DIVISION OF ROULETTE RECORDS, INC.

LP 1146

MY MAN SPEEDY!
JOE CUBA SEXTET

DL 74945 — STEREO

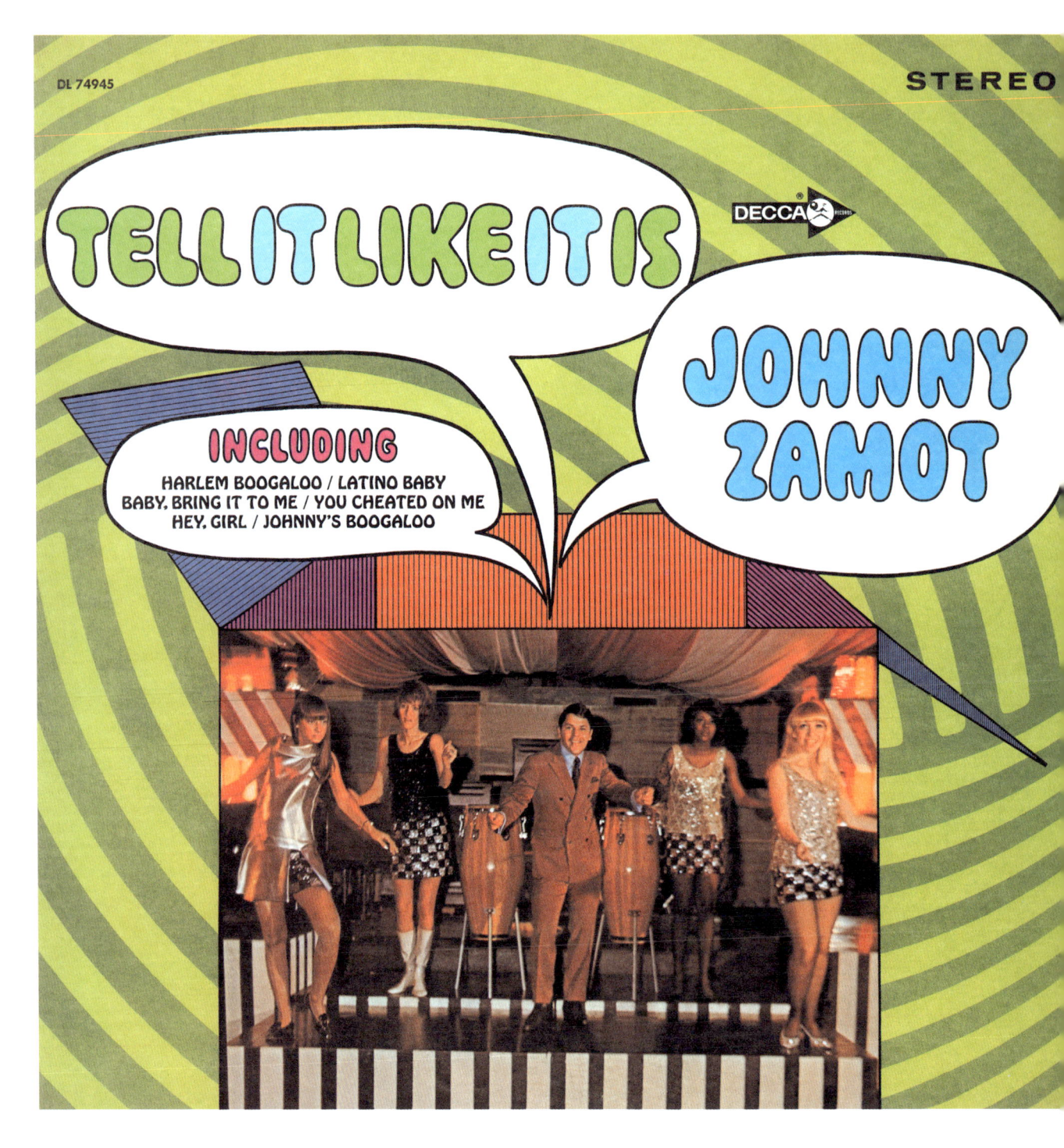

TELL IT LIKE IT IS

JOHNNY ZAMOT

DECCA

INCLUDING
HARLEM BOOGALOO / LATINO BABY
BABY, BRING IT TO ME / YOU CHEATED ON ME
HEY, GIRL / JOHNNY'S BOOGALOO

STEREO CS-1038

The Boys
Sex Symbols
simbolos sexuales

COTIQUE

(S)LP 1172
STEREO
TICO
HIGH FIDELITY
THE KING TITO PUENTE
CHAN
BAN BAN

HIPPIES BOOGALOO

HOPES 885

EDDIE BASTIAN and his Orchestra

FANIA SLP 345 stereo

FANIA RECORDS

JOE BATAAN

SUBWAY

LE-FRISSON

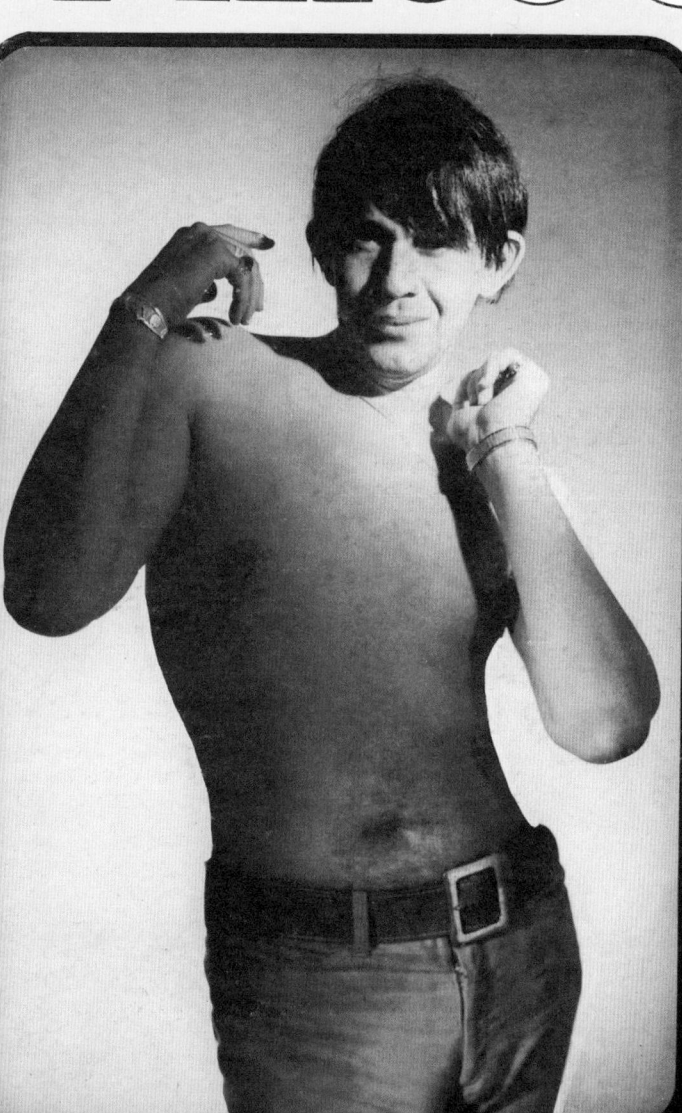

POP ART RECORDS
LP-150

EDUARDO DAVIDSON

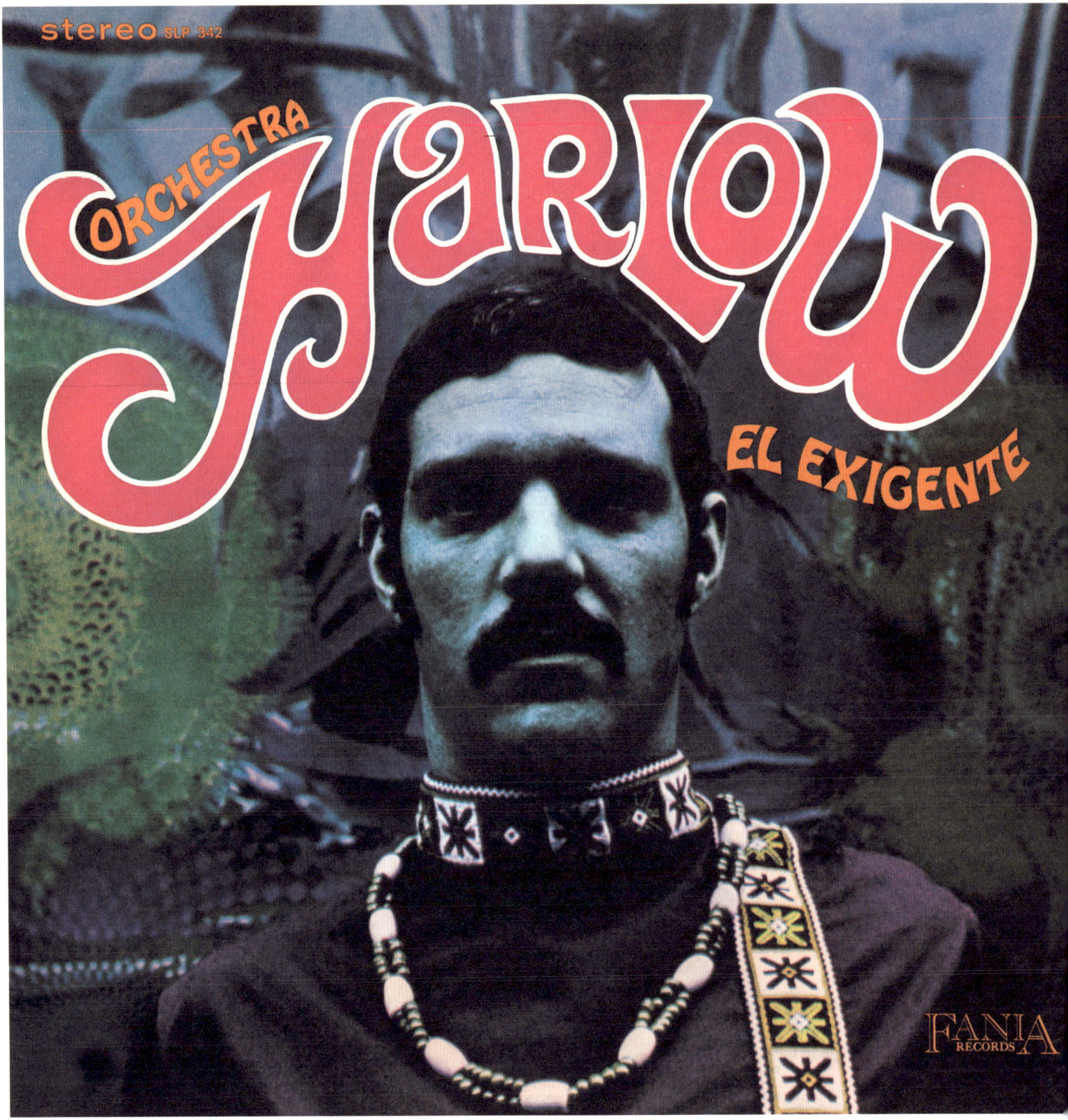
stereo SLP 342
ORCHESTRA
Harlow
EL EXIGENTE
FANIA
RECORDS

CS-1022 stereo

The LeBron Brothers

I BELIEVE

COTIQUE

FANIA SLP 346 stereo

FANIA RECORDS

ACID
RAY BARRETTO

Tiger Boo-Ga-Loo
The Latin Souls

STEREO
KAPP
KS-3553

STEREO
SLP-1194

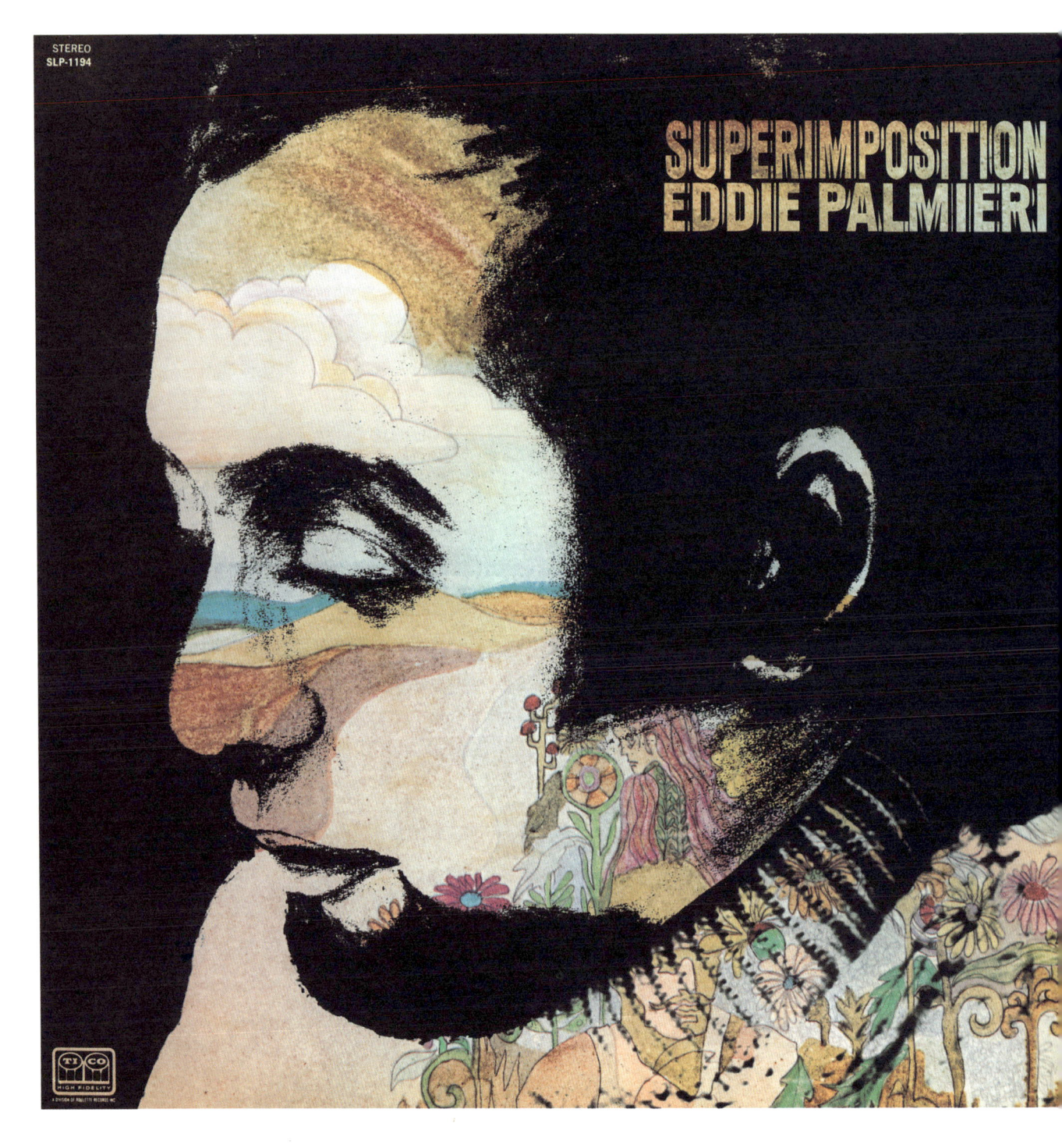

SUPERIMPOSITION
EDDIE PALMIERI

TICO
HIGH FIDELITY

SLP 386 stereo

DE TODO UN POCO

FANIA

MONGUITO
"el unico" y su conjunto

FANIA SLP 379 stereo

THE HARVEY AVERNE BAND/BROTHERHOOD
GOT TO HAVE BROTHERHOOD/RUNAWAY CHILD/STAND/GET BACK/DON'T LET ME DOWN/PEOPLE/
MY DREAM/STRUTTIN' SLOW/LOVERS/COME ON AND DO ME/LOVE NEVER STAYS THE SAME/COME BACK BABY

FANIA

GUISANDO
DOING A JOB
FANIA
WILLIE COLON
CANTA
HECTOR LAVOE
FANIA LP 370 mono

V6-8631 STEREO

spanish grease / willie bobo

Soul Sauce / Cal Tjader

Verve

® © Metro-Goldwyn-Mayer, Inc./Printed in U.S.A.

V-8614

JUSTICIA

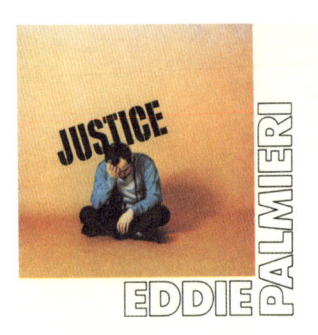

JUSTICE — EDDIE PALMIERI

STEREO
SLP-1188

TICO
HIGH FIDELITY

FANIA SLP 374 **stereo**

ORCH. HARLOW

EVERYBODY'S GOT SOMETHING TO HIDE EXCEPT **ME AND MY MONKEY** "MI MONO Y YO"

FANIA

SLP 1211

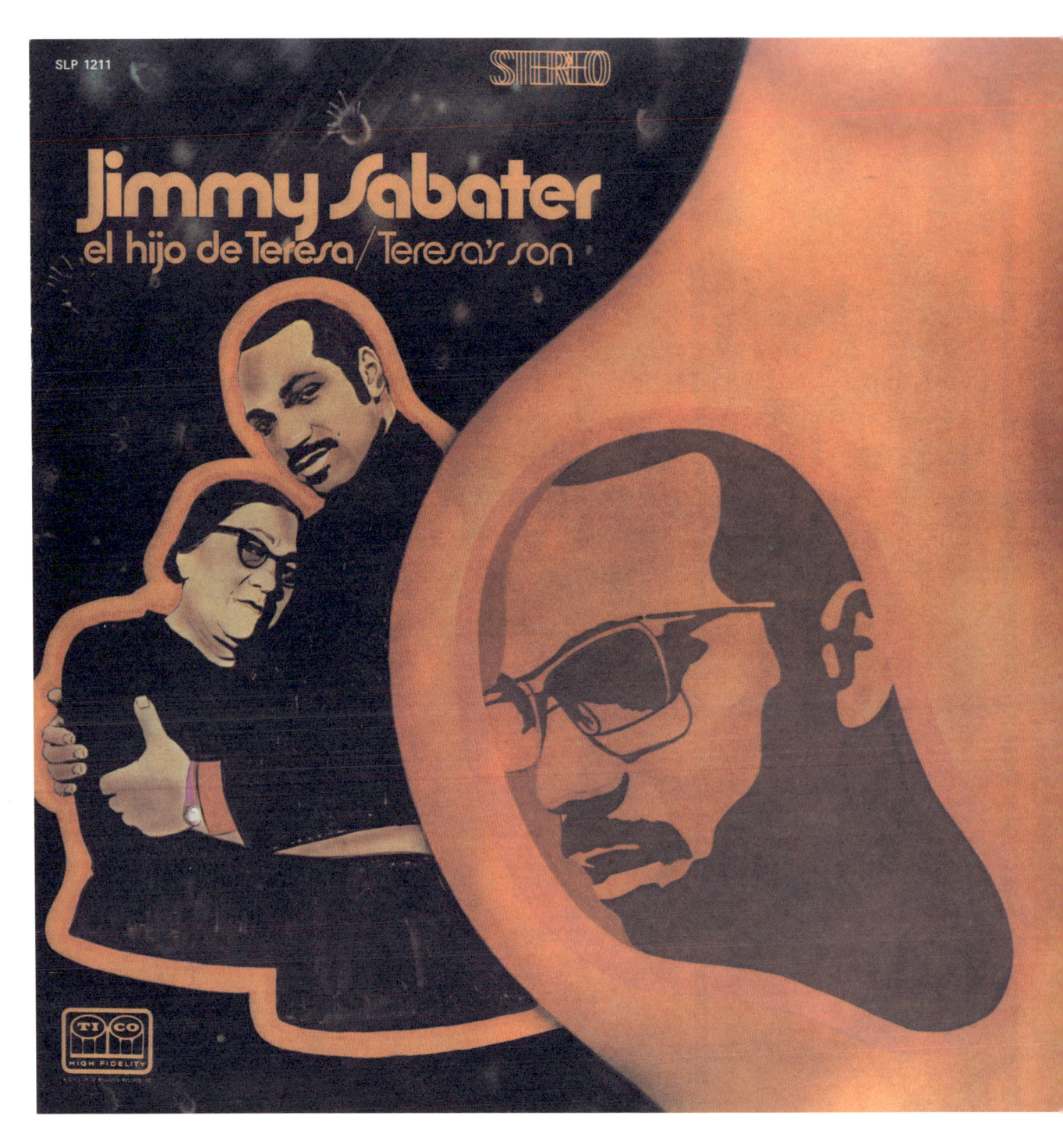

STEREO

Jimmy Sabater
el hijo de Teresa / Teresa's son

TICO
HIGH FIDELITY

MONGO SANTAMARIA
FEELIN' ALRIGHT

STEREO
SD 8252
ATLANTIC

RAY RODRIGUEZ
& his orchestra
Delusion

ALEGRE RECORDS

LPA-869

juicy
WILLIE BOBO

STEREO

V6-8685

willie bobo — uno dos tres 1·2·3

Verve

V-8648

TITO PUENTE EN EL PUENTE
ON THE BRIDGE

TICO HIGH FIDELITY
A DIVISION OF ROULETTE RECORDS INC

LP-1191

Échale Salsita

SALSA

1970s–1980s

This chapter takes its title from the eponymous Cuban standard by Ignacio Piñero, meaning "put a little sauce on it." Salsa emerged from the ashes of boogaloo, but Latin Soul never died, it just transformed. Inspired in part by black America's search for roots and self-determination, and by the heady mix of styles that came out of Spanish Harlem in the 1960s, Nuyoricans investigated authentic Cuban and Puerto Rican sounds, recovering Africanisms and peasant folk traditions, reinventing as they went. This atmosphere of revolution and ethnic pride brought concerns of Latino identity to the forefront and fostered an explosion of experimentation coupled with a new sense of purpose for the jacket as a marker of culture in the expanding Hispanic marketplace. As Harvey Averne comments: "My attitude was, let's go get this music I love out of this *cuchifrito* environment and treat it like every other genre."

It was at this juncture that Jerry Masucci's Fania Records emerged as the dominant force in the industry.

"Jerry always wanted to crossover, to be a success in the white world," says designer Ron Levine, who began working with Fania in 1975. "What Masucci was hoping for when he hired me was to get this rock and roll white boy with long hair dressed in leather to help them compete." Levine, who had extensive experience with mainstream labels, produced a series of pivotal covers for the label, including Willie Colón's *The Good, The Bad, The Ugly*.

Even in this atmosphere of empowerment and burgeoning industry, there were pitfalls for designers. "I used to fight about logo and title sizes, and the printing was atrocious; a lot of the lettering was press type or hand done," said Levine. "The printers didn't have any cool fonts. Photo lettering was expensive but the advantage was it had the most design-oriented type for headlines. All the lines on the covers were painstakingly done with a ruler and rapidograph pen, too expensive for the printers to do in production. A lot of covers were just basically nothing, had to bang them out just to service Fania, there was just such a volume."

The sheer amount of work was staggering, and often led to quality control issues. "Sometimes, when I had a really good idea, it took some convincing," says Sanabria. "I was always bumping heads. Masucci wanted complete control most of the time, but occasionally I was able to turn things around." One cover that made it through was Colón's *La Gran Fuga/The Big Break*, modeled on an FBI "Wanted" poster. "I wanted to play up on the whole gangster image to subvert it," said Sanabria. "I had seen these posters of Bobby Seals, and other Black Panthers who were wanted by the FBI... from that idea, I came up with this album cover. The irony is, the mug shot photos are the cheapest damn photographs ever taken for an album cover. I went to the corner where there was one of these arcades. Four photos for a quarter. I wanted that bad quality. The prison numbers under his mug shot are his previous LP catalog numbers." But the label ran into trouble when the imitation "Wanted" flyer that was inserted in the album was posted all over New York and San Juan. "Willie's grandmother was hysterical," said Sanabria. "They were telling her 'Ay, they want your grandson!'" The FBI quickly stepped in and "stopped the thing in its tracks ... all subsequent printings could only say 'Wanted' without the FBI part." The original is now a collector's item. The tongue-in-cheek follow-up, *El Juicio* (The Judge), features a painting by noted courtroom illustrator Aggie Whelane, and is itself the inspiration for an apocryphal legend that had Colón "arrested" and then "represented" at trial by singer Héctor Lavoe. Taken as a unit, Colón's early album covers trace a cinematic trajectory of the Latino as criminalized outlaw, starting with the street tough (*El Malo*) and petty pool shark (*The Hustler*), graduating to thievery and organized crime (*Guisando/Doing A Job, Cosa nuestra*), leading to the inevitable incarceration (*La Gran Fuga*) and trial (*El Juicio*), and finally culminating with the artist as a hostage-taking terrorist (*Lo mato*).

For Rubén Blades' first joint effort with Colón, *Metiendo a mano* (Making Things Happen), Colón appears as a trainer "presenting" Blades as the new contender to challenge recently departed Lavoe's "title" as the champion *sonero mayor* of salsa. For their next effort, *Siembra* (Sowing), multiracial babies signify, according to Blades, "the hope for the future" implied in the title. "That cover never worked the way I wanted it to," he continues. "The babies were crying, not paying attention. It was the shoot from hell. Then they had all these strange 1970s-type of drawings [by Irene Perlicz] on the side, like Peter Max but in muted earth colors." Nevertheless, it is now an iconic period piece.

In addition to creating visual identities for Colón and Blades, Sanabria created another long-lasting narrative iconology—for Fania bandleader Ray Barretto. Sanabria was interested in empowering Latinos through positive imagery, and *conguero* Barretto was the perfect vehicle. Whether depicted as Sampson for the LP *Power* or breaking the chains of ignorance and prejudice on *Que viva la música*, there was often a revolutionary slant to his depictions of Barretto. "We always worked together," Sanabria said. "Sometimes I had to convince a musician of something that was hard for them to believe in at first. *Indestructible* was a prime example.... When Ray saw the Superman shirt Walter [Velez] made ... he didn't want to do it, he was afraid people were going to goof on him." Sanabria was undeterred. "Ray's black frame glasses were already a part of his image, so my idea was to have him be like Clark Kent, taking them off.... Years later, Ray said to me 'You know Izzy, much as I was afraid of that thing, people come up to me with a smile and thank me for being a Latin superhero.'"

A pop-art sensibility informed many of the most innovative covers from the 1970s, the best example being Sanabria's design for the groundbreaking Latin fusion album *Pura salsa* by Panamanian *sonero* Azuquita. The sugar box alludes to the singer's name (the translation is "little sugar"), as well as "pure stuff" (i.e. cocaine). For Hector Rivera's *Lo máximo* (The Biggest), Walter Velez humorously portrays the normally mild-mannered pianist as a nude King Kong astride a particularly phallic Empire State Building. Larry Harlow directed the design for his 1973 "salsa opera" *Hommy*: "It was supposed to be bananas on one side, oranges on the other, but it didn't come out that way." *Hommy* is sophisticated material—a narrative dance album—and its cover was intended as a plea to understand the individual as a person, and not as a commodity (to make the point, a photograph of Harlow as a baby is screened over an orange).

By the mid-1970s, Fania had achieved its goal of elevating the presentation and packaging of its roster of artists, but that left others on the scene feeling pressured to get out from under the shadow of the salsa giant. Respected trumpeter and influential arranger Joe Cain ran Tico Records for a time during this era, and he felt that fine art and realistic photography would best serve his artists. "I had a lot of power at Tico, so I wanted to upgrade the covers. For too long at Fania you'd look at an album, without even seeing the name of the artist, you knew right away it was a Latin cover. It was cheesy. I had a deep interest and a love for the music and a lot of respect for the musicians. Even with Ely [Besalel], who is a genius, his first stuff, I said 'I don't like it, it looks dull, like you did it in ten minutes!' and he looked at me, we looked at each other... and [after that] he gave me some great albums. My favorite is Ismael Rivera's *Esto fue lo que trajo el barco*."

Cain was also at the helm for several pivotal Joe Cuba albums. With *Bustin' Out*, Besalel created a documentary-style barrio scene in sepia, burned around the edges as if the image had been fished from a trash can. "That was the first time we posed in our street clothes," said Cuba. "I didn't know it was going to be black and white at first, but it showed our new hard style of music." Besalel used graffiti lettering, a technique previously employed by Sanabria, to bring street credibility and signify the band's newfound gritty authenticity (as opposed to the glitz of its Palladium days). "I hated the graffiti on the walls everywhere," says Sanabria, referring to his Ray Barretto cover *Acid*, "but it was a fact of city life; it might have looked like I did it slap-dash, but I labored over it." *Cocinando la salsa*, art directed by Ron Levine, documents another side of Cuba's personality, that of host and cook. "This picture shows me cooking all the good Puerto Rican stuff at a Cuban-Chinese joint on the West Side where we used to hang out and talk and eat." Ron Levine's *Sofrito* cover for Mongo Santamaría also depicts the artist in the kitchen (Mongo is on the back proudly displaying his home-cooked *comida criolla*), capitalizing on the ready culinary metaphors.

Several records in this collection depict actual events in the lives of their creators. Ray Barretto's 1979 comeback album, *Rican/struction*, alludes to the facts that Barretto had just put his old Fania band back together, that he had recovered from a "personal crisis" during a period of musical exploration on other labels, and that acupuncture had alleviated pain in a badly damaged hand. *Rican/struction* was a welcome return to form. On the Dalí-esque cover, Barretto is shown as a mountainous Gulliver while Lilliputian figures toil furiously around him. The design was conceived by an overworked Sanabria, who passed it off to an associate for realization. "I gave Jorge Vargas, a terrific painter, a detailed layout of my idea, and this is what he came up with," said Sanabria. Tragicomic Latin superstar Héctor Lavoe's eerily convincing impression of Charlie Chaplin on his ironically titled solo LP *Comedia* seems to foretell a life story fraught with bad luck, addiction, attempted suicide, and early death from AIDS.

After a (practically required) apprenticeship with Sanabria at Fania, Charlie Rosario, who had studied design at New York's School of Visual Arts, realized he would have more freedom to follow his muse if he left the Fania fold to work for smaller labels. "I just broke away and did my thing," he said. "I was manipulated by some of the labels, I didn't get paid so well; sometimes I feel like an unknown, though my art is in the store twenty-five years later." The designs he produced in the 1970s stand as some of the most creative of the period, and often employ groundbreaking use of mixed media. His cover for Conjunto Melao's debut on TR records is typical of his style. *Melao* is slang for *melado*, the sticky goo that comes from squeezed sugar cane, and also means honey-colored, like mulatto skin. Not surprisingly, it is commonly used as a double-entendre in lusty songs. Here, Rosario literally spells out the group's name with it below a sexually charged still life. For Charlie Palmieri's *ElectroDuro*, he formed a sculptural composition from beer cans, a printing plate, a cracker tin, and more than two hundred painstakingly hammered nails. For *Típica '73's La Candela*, he enlisted his family and friends in the weaving of a tapestry with the album's typography (it was intended as a gatefold). "It took forever, I was freaking out...it was like 'everybody's gonna sew here 'til our eyeballs fall out,'" he said.

The process wasn't always smooth. When an illustration was required for Eddie Palmieri's now classic *The Sun of Latin Music* on short notice, Rosario resurrected an image created and then rejected for a 1970 Ricardo Ray album. The aforementioned *Kako* cover was created on the beach at Coney Island after the original photo shoot—in Rosario's basement—went up in flames. "I built this giant pyramid, dug out a trench, and photographed it looking up so this seven-inch clay sculpture appears huge, monumental."

Ely Besalel got into the act of making three-dimensional cover art with the experimental Coco release *Cortijo and His Time Machine*, which featured a striking surrealist construction that brings to mind the work of Joseph Cornell. Coco president Harvey Averne specifically instructed his designers to avoid head shots: "I wanted to record my heroes from when I was a little Anglo kid infatuated with Latin music....But at a certain point I got tired of having the artists' faces on the covers all the time. I loved and respected them, but how many covers had these guys had their pictures on over the years?"

Charlie Rosario's cousin Yogi Rosario was innovative as well, doing work for Salsoul, Tico, and other labels. Combining his training in commercial art with his skills in drawing and photography, he introduced the collage to Latin record design, of which the Tito Rodriguez reissue *Uptempo* is a fine example. "I always kept a lot of pictures around. I kept a photographic diary of the times, but for Tito I just cut all this stuff out of popular magazines and comics." For the Grupo Folklórico y Experimental Nuevayorquino's *Lo dice todo*, Rosario traveled with the band taking photographs, and then produced a collage of instruments taken from children's books. The music was a collection of authentic sounds from Cuba and Puerto Rico brought together in an unprecedented fashion; according to Yogi, he wanted the cover to proudly proclaim "This is *our* music!" Both that disk and the award-winning debut, *Concepts in Unity* (also a Rosario production), were luxury gatefold albums with extensive liner notes—firsts for folkloric recordings.

Eddie Palmieri's 1978 album *Lucumí, Macumba, Voodoo*, a masterful weaving of dance-floor grooves and sacred music, marked his move from the minor-leagues of Latin recording to a major label: CBS. But Palmieri still managed to be subversive, and the album's design can be seen as an attempt to "out" the misunderstood Afro-Atlantic New World religions of the title. Here, a model bears a swanlike neck to reveal an array of *lucumí collares*, the necklaces worn by the *orishas*, or spirit beings, of the Afro-Cuban religion *santería*. The obvious grace and sophistication of her Madison Avenue bearing enhance rather than detract from the markers of traditional faith at her throat. What's more, these multicolored coded beads are numbered and then described in the album's extensive liner notes. The art director was a young Paula Scher, who would become the first female partner at the noted design firm Pentagram.

In contrast with the sophistication and glamour of the New York scene, Venezuelan superstar Oscar d'Leon gives us the *salsero* as Olympian athlete. The sports figure has always loomed large in minority communities as a representation of power, expertise, pride, and escape from poverty. In this low budget shot for *El discóbolo*, d'Leon shows that his athletic strength is matched by his power to earn gold records.

Many of the covers in this chapter challenged standard conventions for the representation of Latino identity. It makes sense to conclude with a comparison of approaches to this problem. Both were produced for Sonora Ponceña, a native Puerto Rican band that plays classic salsa with a distinctly *típico* flavor. The first, the eponymous *Sonora Ponceña*, is a product of the Sanabria (design) and Velez (illustration) team, and features a deluxe-style depiction of Ponce de Leon in full body armor carrying a guitar and a maraca. When Ron Levine took over for the Inca label, there was some controversy about how the group should be packaged. Sanabria had always been a booster of message covers, and while he acknowledged that Ron's art was "beautiful," he took issue with the fact that it "misrepresents the music and culture inside." But for Levine, the essential ghettoization implicit in the deluxe style was the problem itself: "To the Latin world, the gringo rock and roll and R&B covers represented bands that were making tons of money while the salsa guys, who were just as good at their craft, were making crap." Levine's science-fiction and fantasy covers put Latin music on the same plane as major mainstream artists like Boston, ELO, and Yes. "It's all about dollars in and dollars out," he says. "The art had nothing to do with the music, they were just mood pieces."

XSLP #00484
SERIES 0598
compatible **stereo**

THE GOOD
THE BAD
THE UGLY

FANIA

WANTED BY FBI

For: THE BIG BREAK – La Gran Fuga
WILLIE COLON
Alias: EL MALO · THE HUSTLER

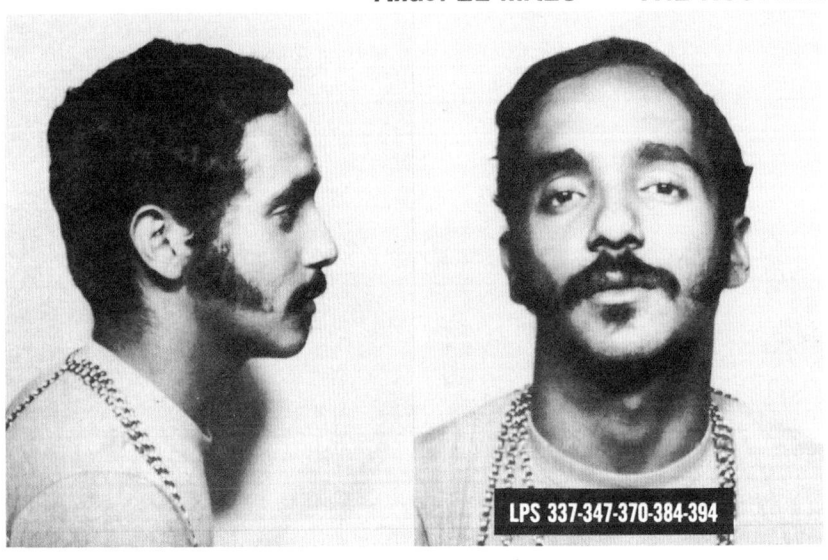

LPS 337-347-370-384-394

ARMED WITH TROMBONE AND CONSIDERED DANGEROUS

WILLIE COLON was last seen in New York City, he may be accompanied by one, HECTOR LaVOE, occupation "singer", also a very dangerous man with his voice.

CRIMINAL RECORD

These men are wanted by the dancing public. They are responsible for hit records such as: Che Che Cole, Guisando, Oiga Senor, Juana Pena, Jazzy and I Wish I Had a Watermelon.

CAUTION

Willie Colon and Hector LaVoe have been known to kill people with little provocation with their exciting rhythm without a moment's notice.

A word to the wise: These men are highly dangerous in a crowd and are capable of starting riots, people immediately start to dance, SO DO NOT, I repeat DO NOT let Hector LaVoe fool you with his smooth style of singing. If you do, you will find yourself dancing a HOLE in your last pair of Shoes.

If anyone knows the whereabouts of Willie Colon and his gang do not notify us. Go immediately to where they are and enjoy yourself.

J. Edgar Gonzalez
J. Edgar Gonzalez
Director F.B.I.
Freaks Bureau of Investigation
Bronx, New York

1.—Right Thumb	2.—R. Index Finger	3.—R. Middle Finger	4.—R. Ring Finger	5.—R. Little Finger
6.—Left Thumb	7.—L. Index Finger	8.—L. Middle Finger	9.—L. Ring Finger	10.—L. Little Finger

FANIA

Album Design: Izzy Sanabria

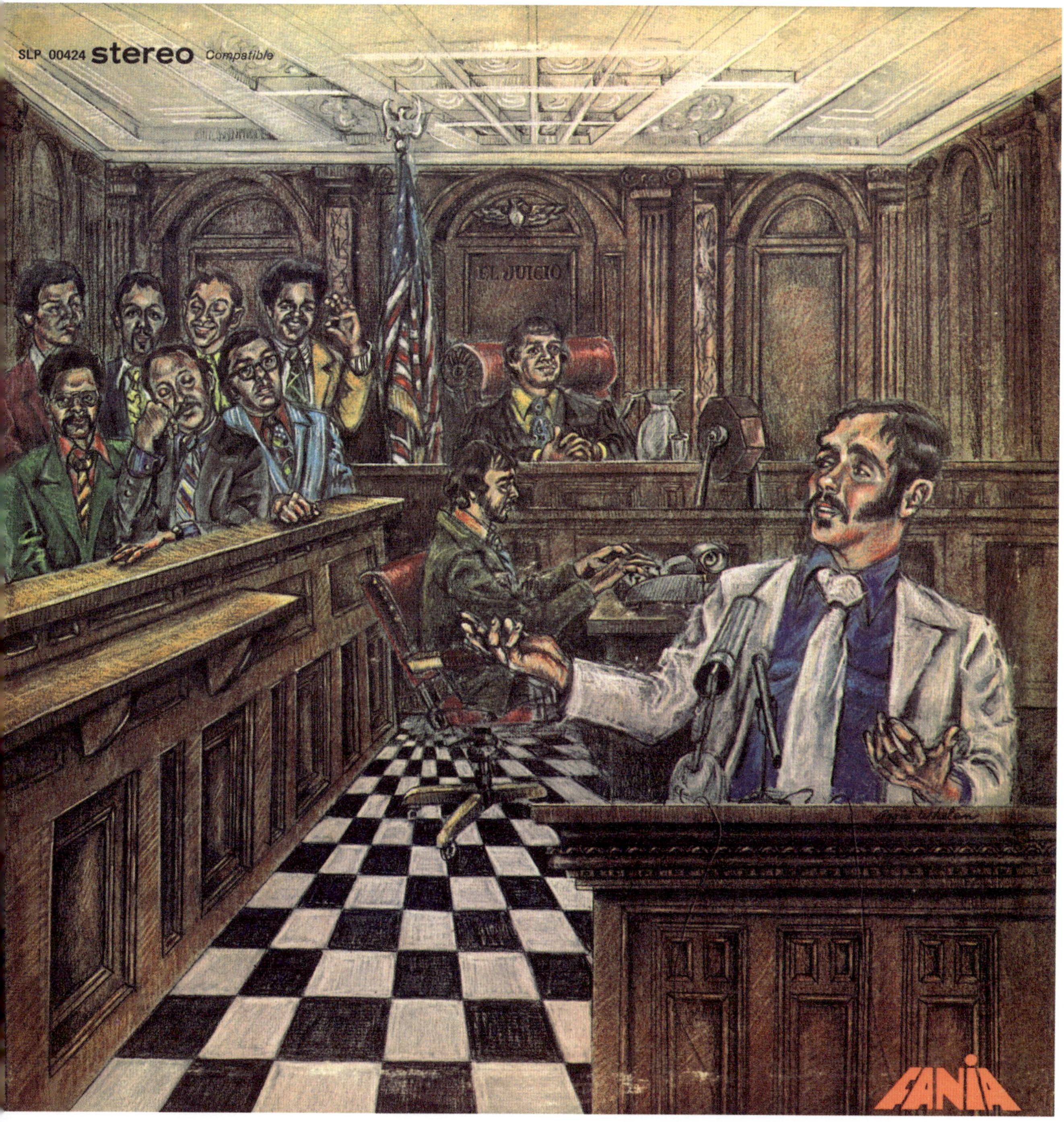
SLP 00424 stereo Compatible
EL JUICIO
FANIA

WILLIE COLON PRESENTS **RUBEN BLADES**

METIENDO MANO!

JMOO-537
SERIES 0698
COMPATIBLE STEREO
SIEMBRA
WILLIE COLON & RUBEN BLADES

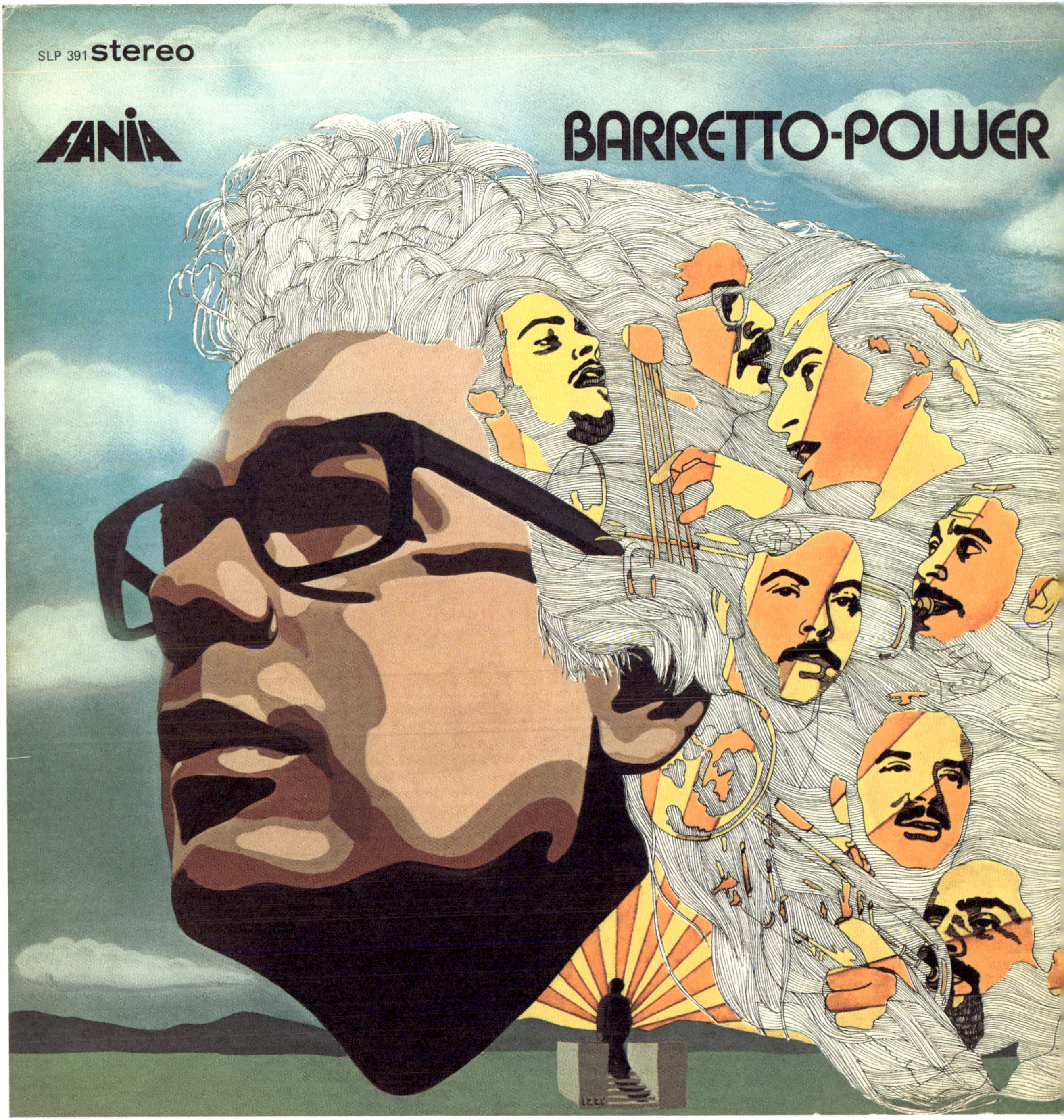
SLP 391 stereo
FANIA
BARRETTO-POWER

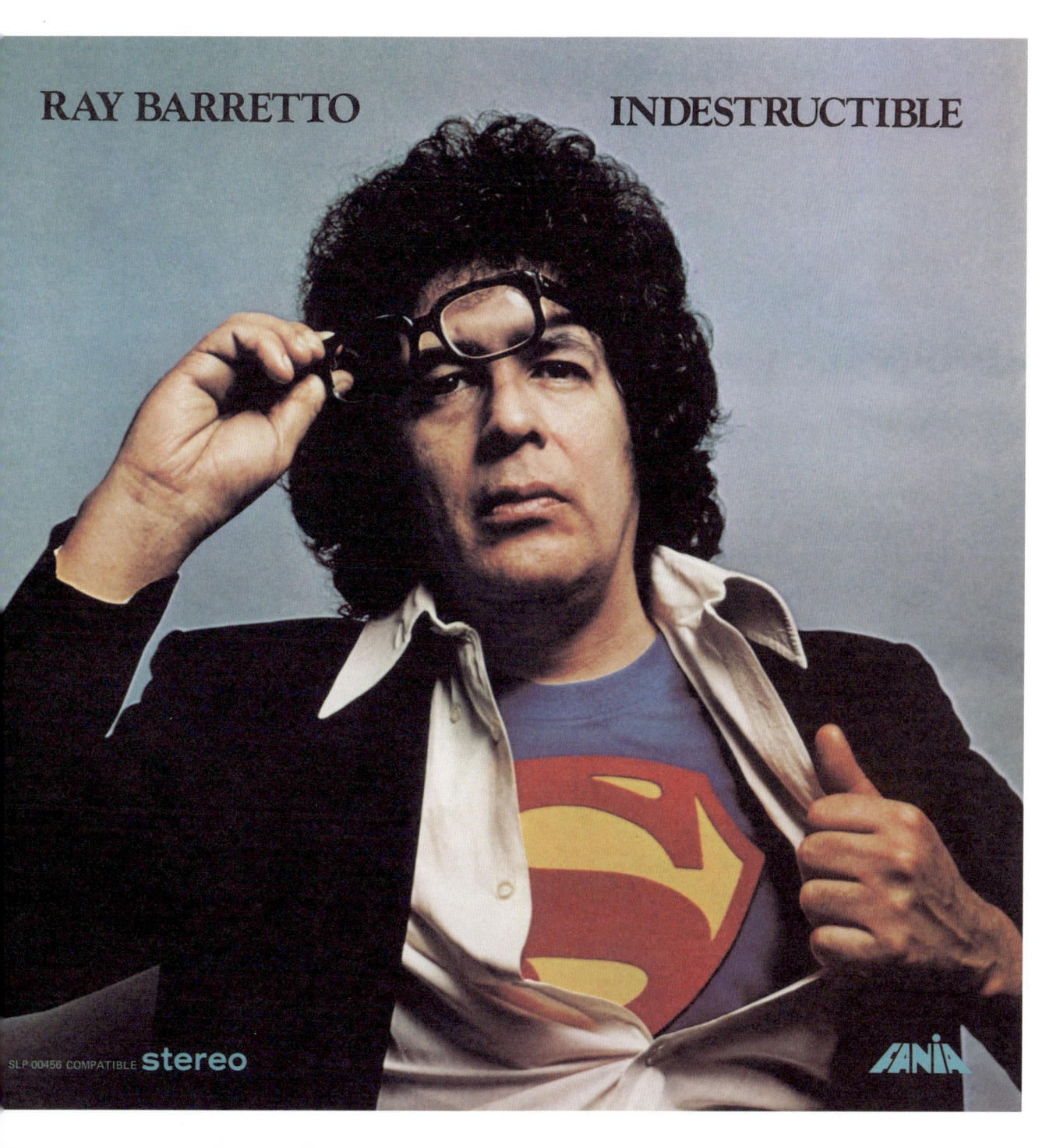

RAY BARRETTO   INDESTRUCTIBLE

SLP 00456 COMPATIBLE **stereo**

fania

RAY BARRETTO/QUE VIVA LA MUSICA

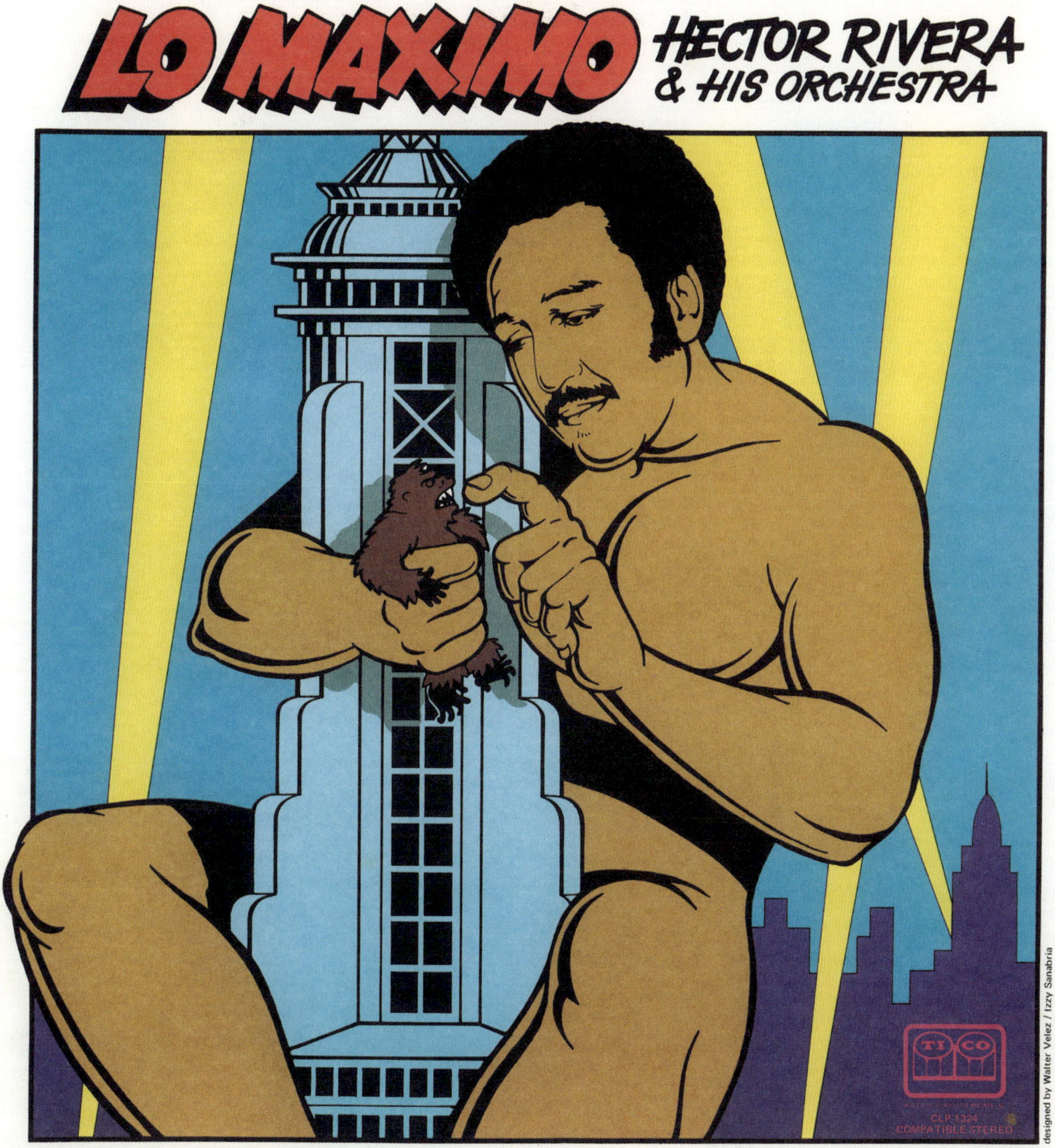

designed by Walter Velez / Izzy Sanabria

Azuquita
POUR SPOUT
Azuquita
Y SU ORQUESTA
PURA SALSA MELAO
CALIFORNIA
COCO DE MARÍA
SALSA NA' MA'
CUARTO BATE
GUAJIRO BACÁN
EN CASA SIÑA JACINTA
SALUDO A PANAMÁ
EL TRANQUILO
VAYA RECORDS INC
Azuquita
Y SU ORQUESTA
PURA SALSA MELAO
NET WT. HEAVY (1 LB)
SALSA RECIPE ON BACK

Ralphy Santi

Y SU CONJUNTO

TR 132X

orchestra harlow
HOMMY
a latin opera

THE JOE CUBA SEXTET

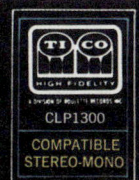

Bustin' Out

TICO HIGH FIDELITY
CLP1300
COMPATIBLE STEREO-MONO

THIS LP INCLUDES JOE CUBA'S X-RATED (Restricted for Radio) VERSION OF PUD-DA-DIN

COPYRIGHT © 1972 TICO RECORDS

JMTS-1405
SERIES 0698
COMPATIBLE STEREO

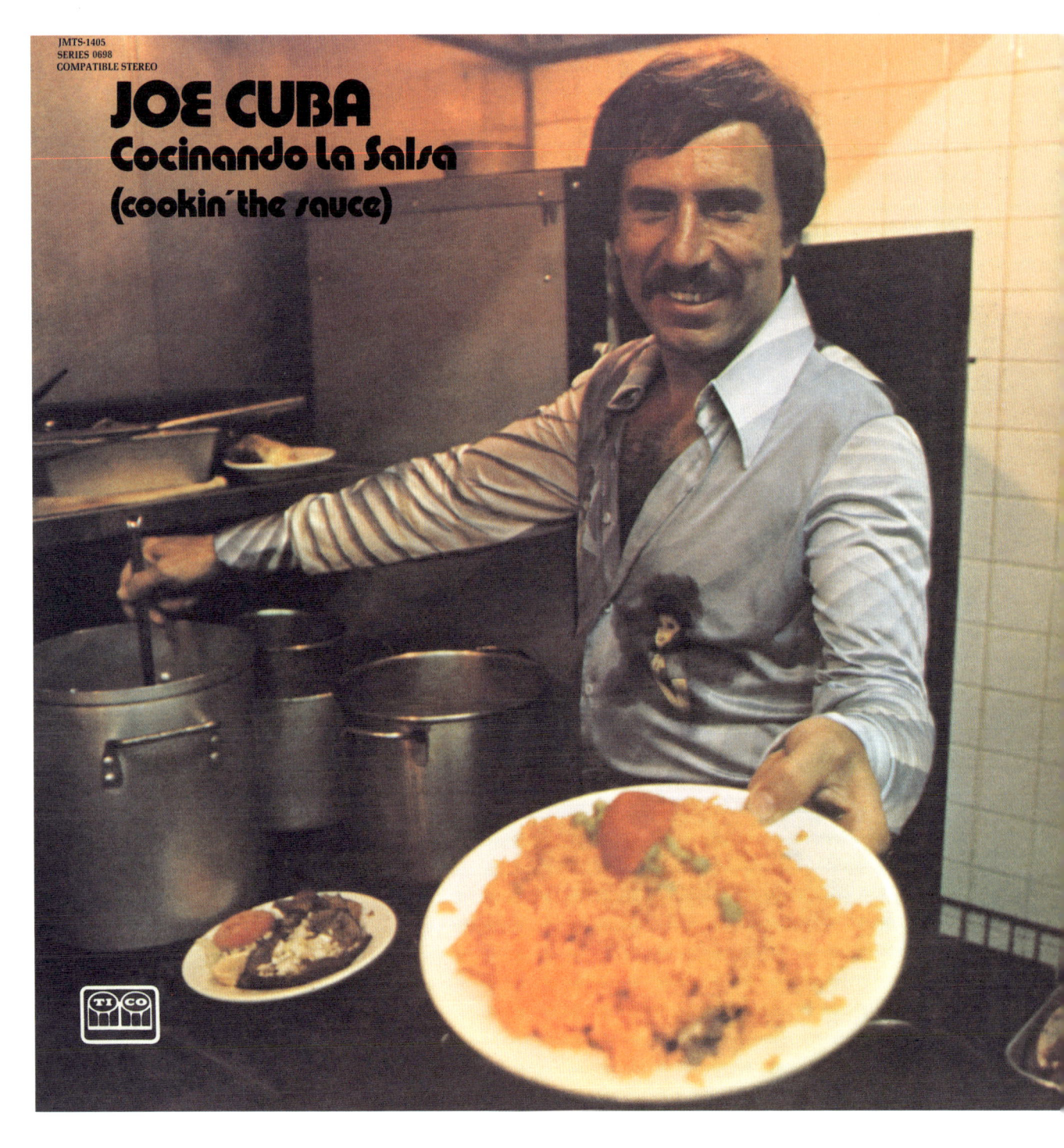

JOE CUBA
Cocinando La Salsa
(cookin' the sauce)

TICO

MONGO SANTAMARIA
SOFRITO

HECTOR LAVOE
COMEDIA

JM-00522
Series 0698
Compatible Stereo

BARRETTO

RICAN/STRUCTION
con ADALBERTO SANTIAGO

EDDIE PALMIERI
THE SUN OF LATIN MUSIC
CLP-109XX
coco records
COMPATIBLE STEREO

KAKO

RECORDS
T.L.P. 00900X
COMPATIBLE STEREO

CHARLIE PALMIERI
ElectroDuro

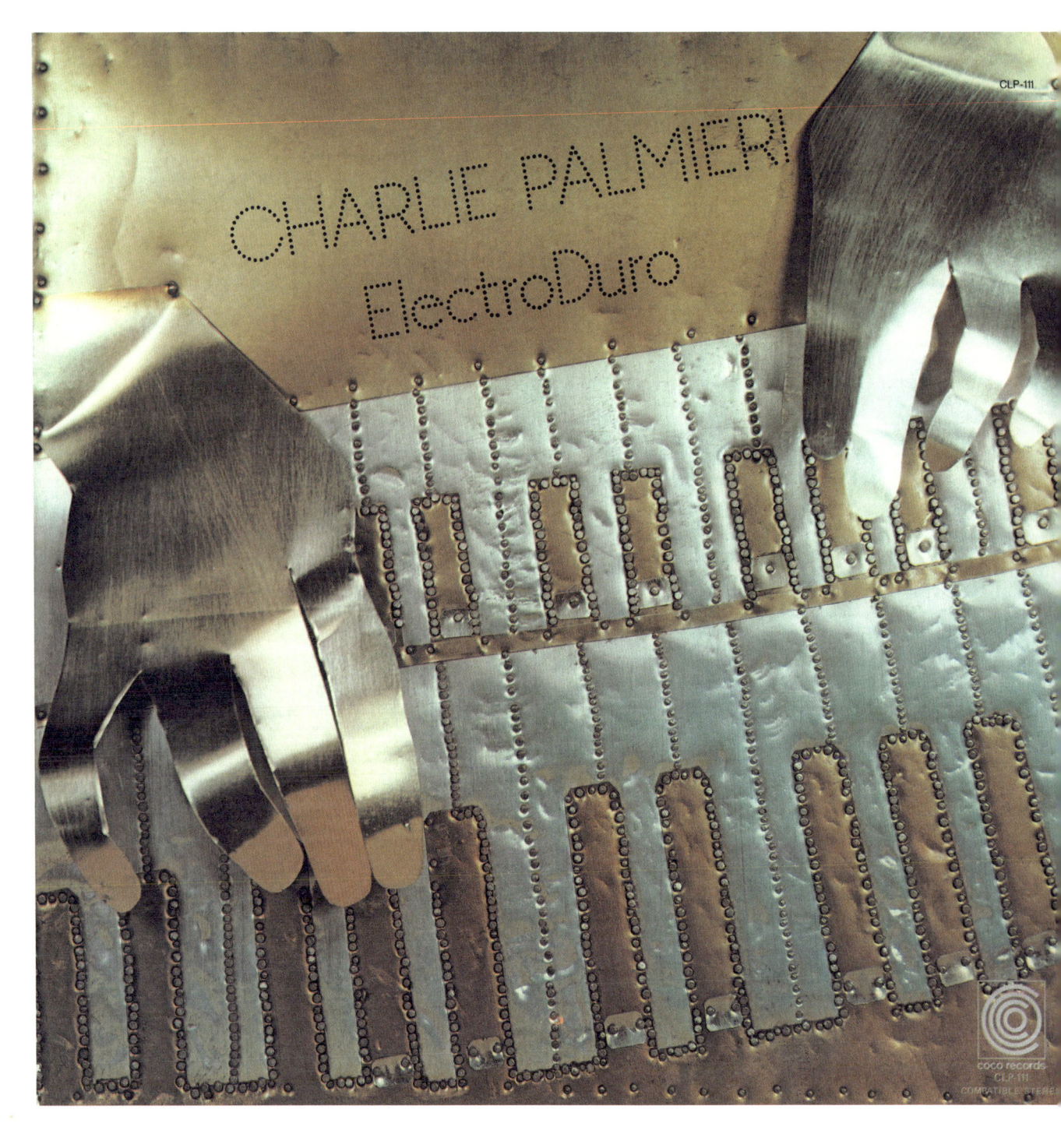

CLP-111

coco records
CLP-111
COMPATIBLE STEREO

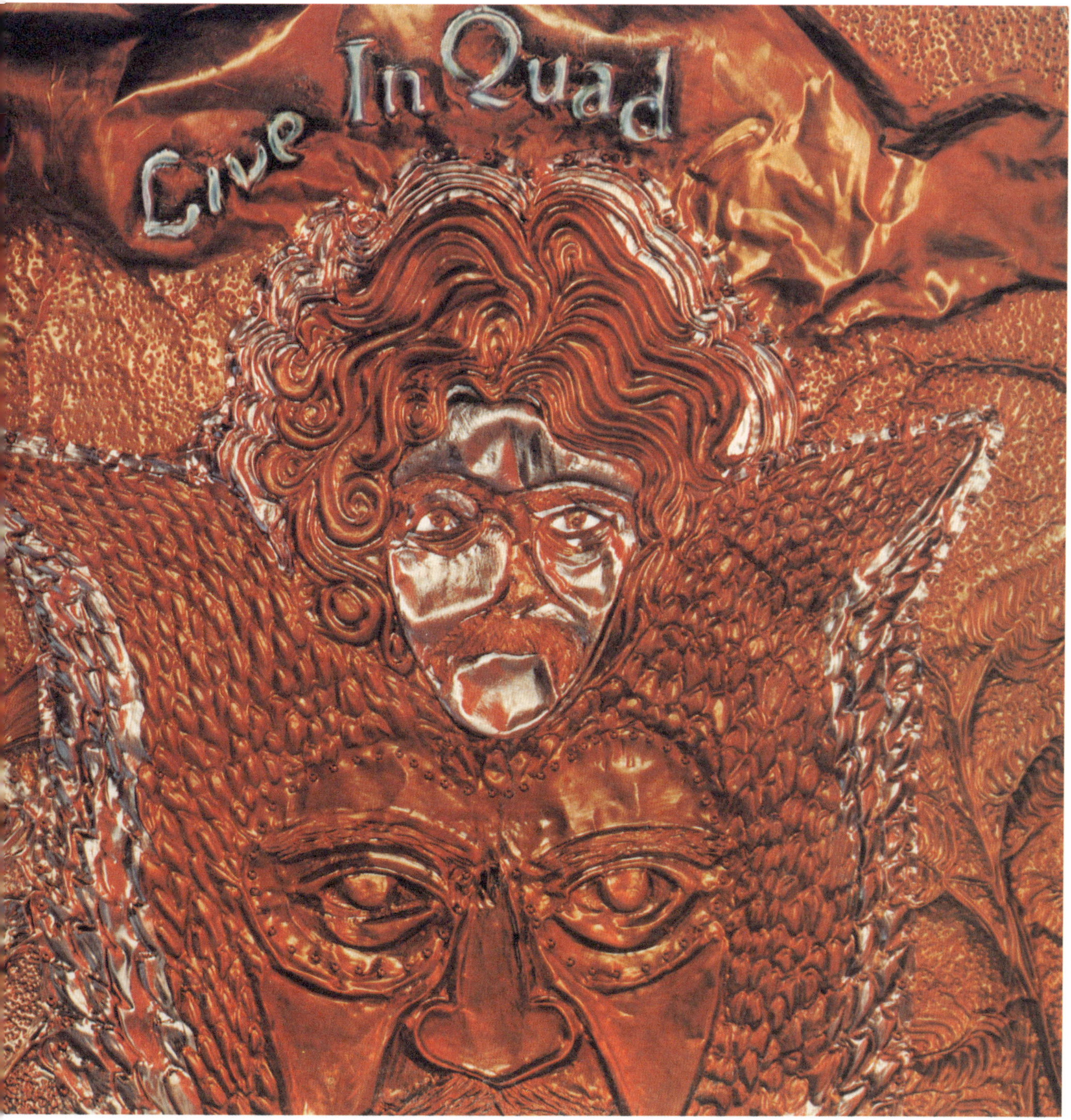
Live In Quad

Conjunto MELAO

T.R. RECORDS 113X
COMPATIBLE STEREO

típica

XSLP-1043
COMPATIBLE
stereo
SERIES 0598

Cortijo & His Time Machine
y su Maquina del Tiempo

CLP 108

coco records
COMPATIBLE STEREO

ISMAEL
RIVERA
CON SUS CACHIMBOS

ESTO
FUÉ
LO QUE
TRAJO
EL BARCO

CLP 1305
COMPATIBLE
STEREO-MONO

TITO RODRIGUEZ
& his orchestra
UPTEMPO

Grupo Folklorico y Experimental Nuevayorquino
"Lo dice todo"

EDDIE
PALMIERI
LUCUMI
MACUMBA
VOODOO

1 Yemaya
2 Eleggua
3 Olla
4 Chango
5 Oggun
6 Ochun
7 Obatala
8 Babalualle

No. 116

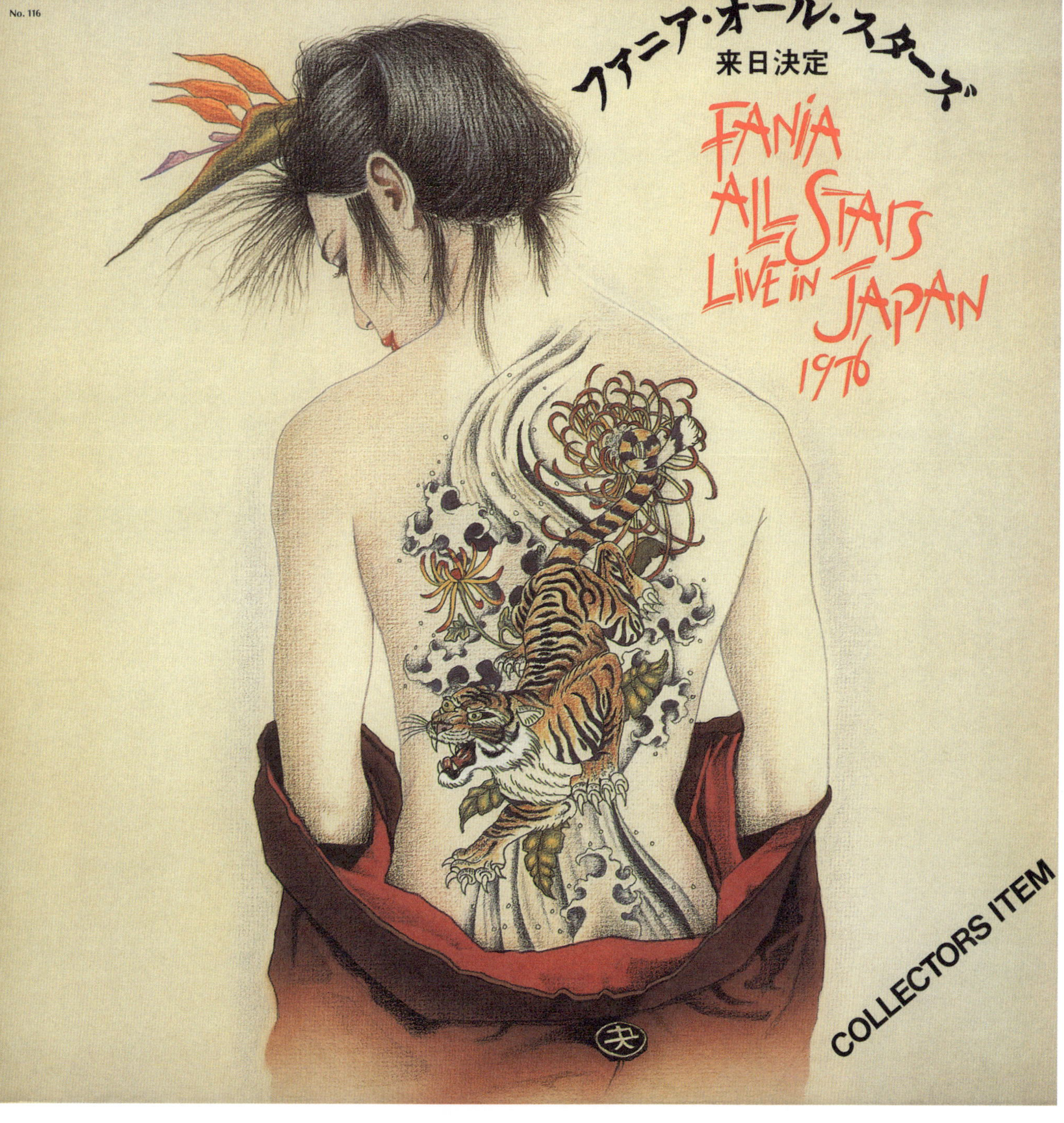
ファニア・オール・スターズ
来日決定
FANIA ALL STARS LIVE IN JAPAN 1976
COLLECTORS ITEM

OSCAR DLEON

El Discóbolo

TH-AMF / 2207
STEREO

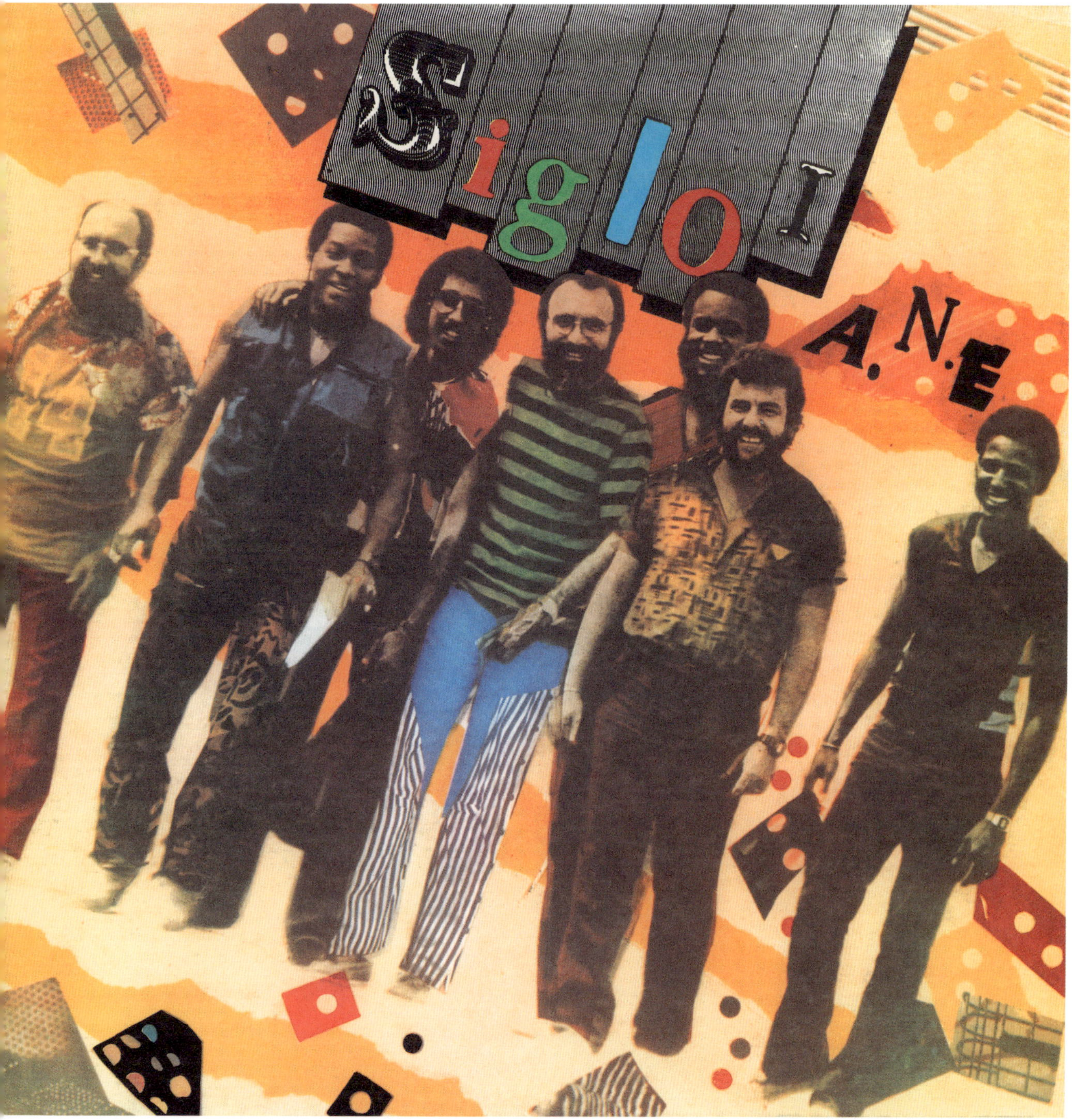
Siglo I
A.N.E

COMPATIBLE stereo SLP 1033

Sonora Ponceña

JMIS-1072 Series 0798 Compatible Stereo

SONORA PONCEÑA
Energized

OYE COMO VA

LATIN ROCK 1960s–1970s

> The Santana crossover just took the business to some whole other level.... It lit a fire under our ass. —Izzy Sanabria

Though the 1970s was the heyday of salsa, Latin sounds were also expanding into other musical genres. As historian David Toop has noted, Latin rock was a "panethnic" utopian movement that "mixed funk with jazz, post-psychedelic rock, African, and Latin elements." Mandrill, War, and Malo are a few of the bands that pioneered this new sound, but the undisputed leader of the movement was Carlos Santana.

Santana's eponymous first album, which opens this chapter, is an exercise in hidden imagery. Much like the popular visual puzzles from the Victorian era or the obsessive illusionism of Salvador Dalí, Bay Area graphic artist Lee Conklin created a multilayered work based on his psychedelic rock posters for Bill Graham's Fillmore West. Decoding the image, we find a black woman inside the mouth of a roaring African lion. She cradles her breasts, emphasizing her fertility and sensuality, while other figures scream or open their mouths, in pain or ecstasy—perhaps in emulation of Santana's self-described "guitar cry."

For his album *Abraxas*, Santana acquired a painting by Mati Klarwein, master of sexually charged, Orientalist kitsch. Here, the artist harnesses his libidinous energy to the brush (his nude models were sexual conquests) and elevates the exotic odalisques of Gauguin and Renoir to the position of Virgin Mother. The Annunciation is communicated through a conga instead of a trumpet (the elephant, meanwhile, is a Buddhist reference). The album was a smash success, although Klarwein—who's work was appropriated by Miles Davis, among other musicians—has remained largely unknown.

Back in the real world, Eddie Palmieri's 1971 masterpiece *Harlem River Drive* appropriates an iconic image by Magnum photographer and civil rights movement chronicler Leonard Freed. Shot on the hot summer streets of Harlem in 1963, the photograph depicts two kids in a fire hydrant's cooling spray. The contrast of the photograph was blown out in the studio of designer Ruby Mazur, enhancing the already dramatic spray lines. Mazur was responsible for an early version of the famous Rolling Stones lips and tongue logo (a deluxe design if ever there was one) initially created by John Pasche in 1971 and also worked on by Sanabria's WE-2 Graphic Designs. Now based in Las Vegas, Mazur paints commissioned portraits of pets.

Again on the streets of uptown Manhattan, we have the front half of a gatefold spread for Harvey Averne's *Barrio Band* made up of the cream of Fania's young generation of salsa musicians, here trying their hand at the Santana sound and pulling it off with a certain Nuyorican twist. This was Averne's one and only release for his fledgling Heavy Duty Records imprint, and it is a sought after collector's item today. While Izzy liked doing the type selection and layout, it was Harvey's baby. "We did the recording, then when I was on vacation in Italy I saw this painting that was perfect." Averne says he wanted to do a documentary shot of the band in their gritty barrio environment for the back of the gatefold. "When I got back we went up to Harlem—me, Izzy, Ralphi Pagán and some guys in the band—and set up this shoot on the stoop, kind of like 'life imitates art,'" said Averne.

Out of the slums of New York's urban ghetto came many an incredible sound, but none so searing as Jimmy Castor's wailing sax and charging timbales. The break beats on this 1972 debut album shaped the sounds of early hip hop DJs of Caribbean heritage including Charlie Chase, Grand Master Flash, and Afrika Bambaataa. In yet another evocation of the bleak urban landscape that enveloped much of New York in the 1970s, we see the leader of the Bunch literally growing out of the tenements with an apocalyptic mushroom cloud as a backdrop. Acy Lehman, designer of the great Willie Bobo, Cal Tjader, and Patato albums for Verve, art directed the painting by the artist Corrigan. As the comically earnest liner notes would have it: "The illustration depicts Jimmy in a double role: as a Gemini and Cancer personality. Gemini aspects are described as egocentric, intellectual, and airy. Castor's egocentric character is affirmed by his unconcealed face; his intellect is symbolized by the tube running from a fitting on his temple to a fitting in the musical tree. His mind drives his music. A second tube runs on to a small cluster of clouds hovering near Castor's head, symbolizing his airy and mutable nature. Castor's Cancer aspects are symbolized on the right by the slum tenement which rises out of wasteland." In the Age of Aquarius, one's sign mattered.

The mandrill, a striking African primate that shares many characteristics with humans, seemed a natural choice for the visual identity of the band of the same name. Though many of the group's covers employ spacey, surreal, and folk art paintings depicting their mascot, 1975's *Solid* stands out with its rock/island aesthetic and dynamically rendered title and sunset. The painting, by Papio Sphinx, came from a concept by the band and veteran art director Bob Cato. Fania's answer to Mandrill, Seguida, debuted with a similarly themed cover painting airbrushed by Sanabria. "*Seguida* means 'right on' or 'straight ahead,' so I put [in] all these perspective lines." For Mongo Santamaría's funk album *Afro-Indio*, Ron Levine produced a masterful watercolor of ritualistic imagery. The Egyptian temple and Massai warrior references echo contemporary Earth, Wind, and Fire packaging, setting it firmly in the mainstream. Levine describes the cover as "complicated yet primitive. It has a symmetry that you get in the music; Mongo's African roots are very strong and the picture worked well for his image."

Meanwhile, a host of bands that built upon the rock foundations of the 1960s, and in particular the seminal sounds of Ritchie Valens, emerged in East L.A. Many did not initially include salsa in their repertoires, and were uncomfortable with the term *Chicano*, (they preferred *Mexican-American*). But, increasingly, the imagery in their music and on their record covers expressed racial pride and support for human rights and workers' issues.

Eddie Caballero's photomontage for El Chicano's 1971 album *Revolución* inserts the band into a revolutionary scene recalling Mexico's liberators of yore, Emiliano Zapata and Francisco "Pancho" Villa. The only hint of color amidst the sepia-toned ruins is an American flag, battle-torn and flaccid. The album contains several anthems, including "Don't Put Me Down (If I'm Brown)." As the historians David Reyes and Tom Waldman have written, "there need[ed] to be an acknowledgment of the Chicano condition if the bands expect[ed] to be taken seriously. The change was abrupt and wholesale."

Covers for El Chicano's *Celebration* and Azteca's *Pyramid of the Moon* also feature symbols of Mexican heritage, though the music contained therein is decidedly fusion in character (*Celebration* features spanglish covers of Van Morrison, Miles Davis, and Cream). For Malo, led by Jorge Santana (brother of Carlos), art director Chris Whorf chose a Meso-American illustration by Jesus Helguera. But the designs of these albums signify that their music is made for *la raza*, and that images like an Aztec princess and an Indian shaman should be acknowledged as much as the low-rider and the zoot suit.

A prime example of regressive self-deprecating racist kitsch comes from the Mexican band Bwana, who employed a deluxe cover with a cartoon *negrito* hippie banging the bongos. (The same image was used on a Brazilian boogaloo album from this period.) The reissue of this album, which has recently enjoyed something of a renaissance, was endowed with a less provocative (though still politically incorrect) cover painting by Mati Klarwein. Adjacent to the original here is Cándido's *Thousand Finger Man*—a cover with an actual black conga master in action.

The chapter closes with a juxtaposition of simple, bold images that convey diametrically opposed messages. On Toro's eponymous heavy metal/salsa record, art directed by Sanabria with typography by Velez and layout by Chico Alvarez, the band's name is fashioned into a confrontationally brutish bull's head logo floating on a sea of blood-red ink. Contrasting with this stark vision of macho virility, Santana's famed *Greatest Hits* cover is a vision of peace, sacrifice, and bi-racial identity, as well as a powerful metaphor for the crossover *mestizo* quality of the music. The award-winning design was the work of Columbia's John Berg, who can still recall the day of its making: "There was a product meeting at Columbia, and I refused to attend those things, but suddenly a girl showed up from the meeting, and said 'they want to do a Santana *Greatest Hits* package, and they want to do it now!' So I ran down the hall, picked up this promotional poster by Joel Baldwin that one of my staff had tacked up on the wall, took it up there, they all loved the photo, and that was the end of that. . . . I didn't want to put any text on it, and probably because it was such a powerful cover, I got away with a sticker instead."

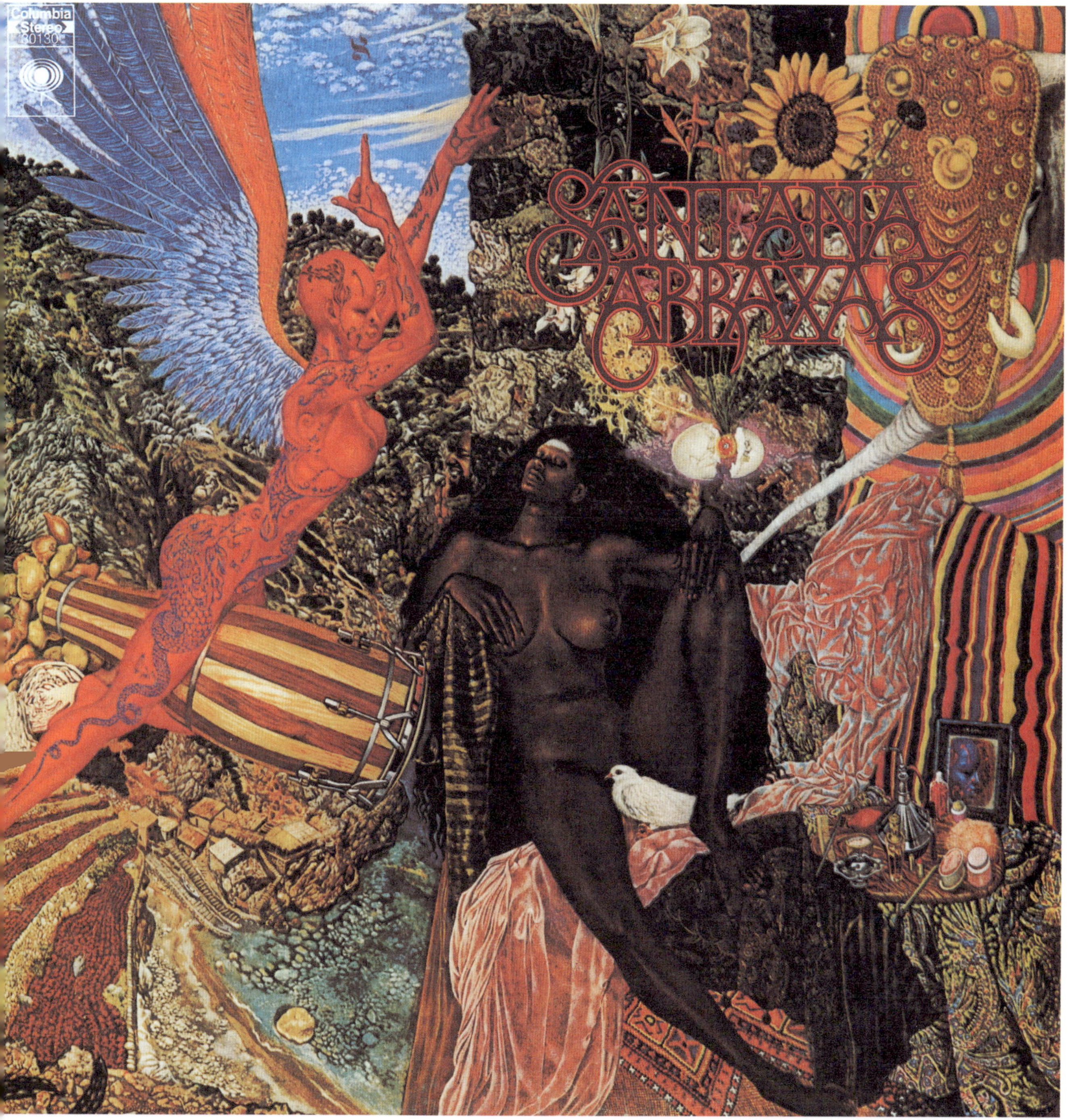
Columbia
Stereo
30130
SANTANA
ABRAXAS

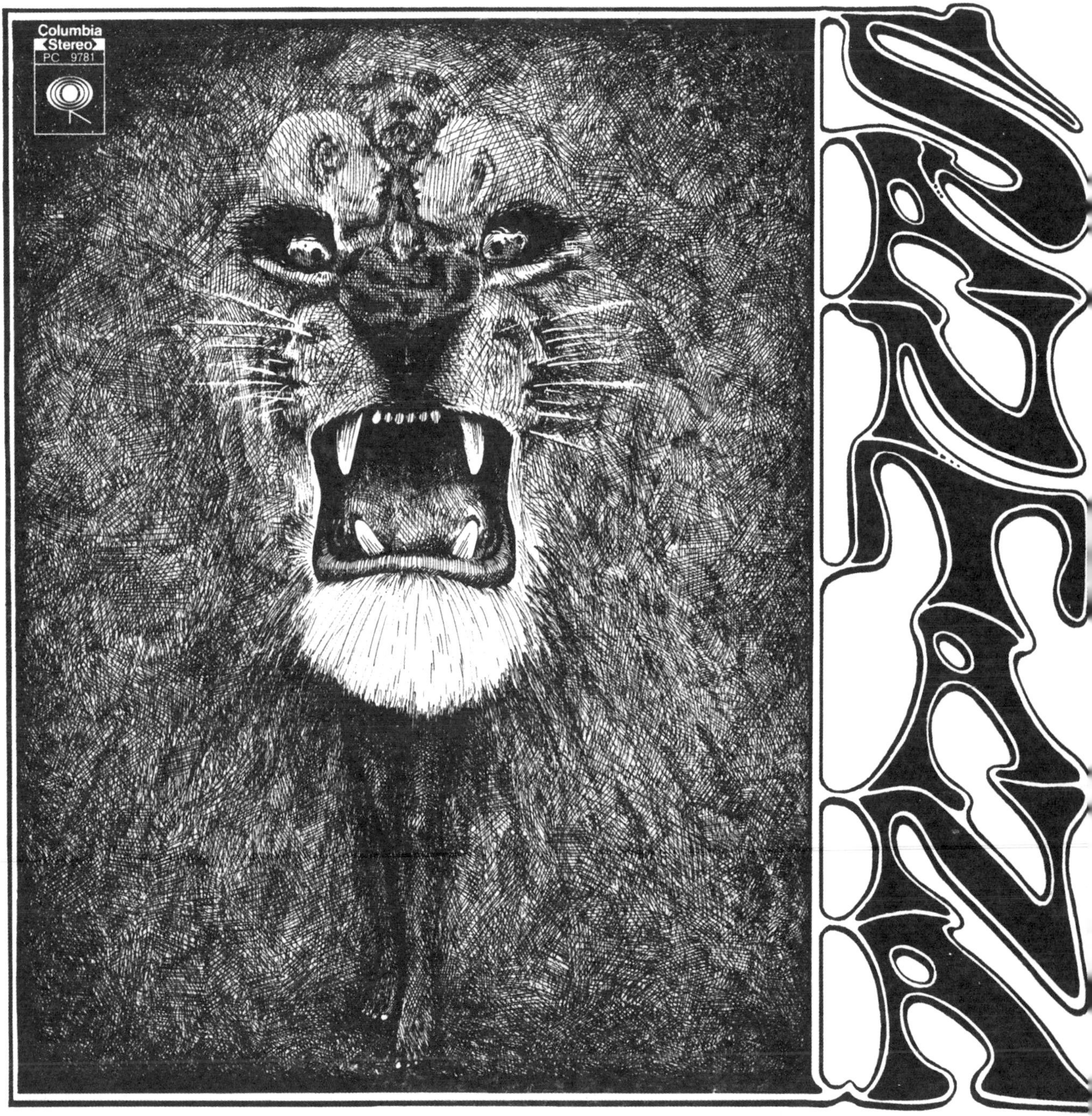
Columbia
Stereo
PC 9781

HARLEM RIVER DRIVE

The
HARVEY
AVERNE
BARRIO
BAND

P 101-STEREO
The HARVEY AVERNE BARRIO BAND
LITTER
ECOLOGY
WASTE
POLLUTION
REPRISA
VIOLENCE
REVOL-A
UTION
URBAN-
IZATION
HEAVY DUTY RECORDS

THE JIMMY CASTOR BUNCH
IT'S JUST BEGUN
RCA
LSP-4640 STEREO
VICTOR

Mandrill
SOLID

COMPATIBLE **stereo**
series 0598

FANIA

Love is... Seguida

XVS-38 series 0598 COMPATIBLE STEREO

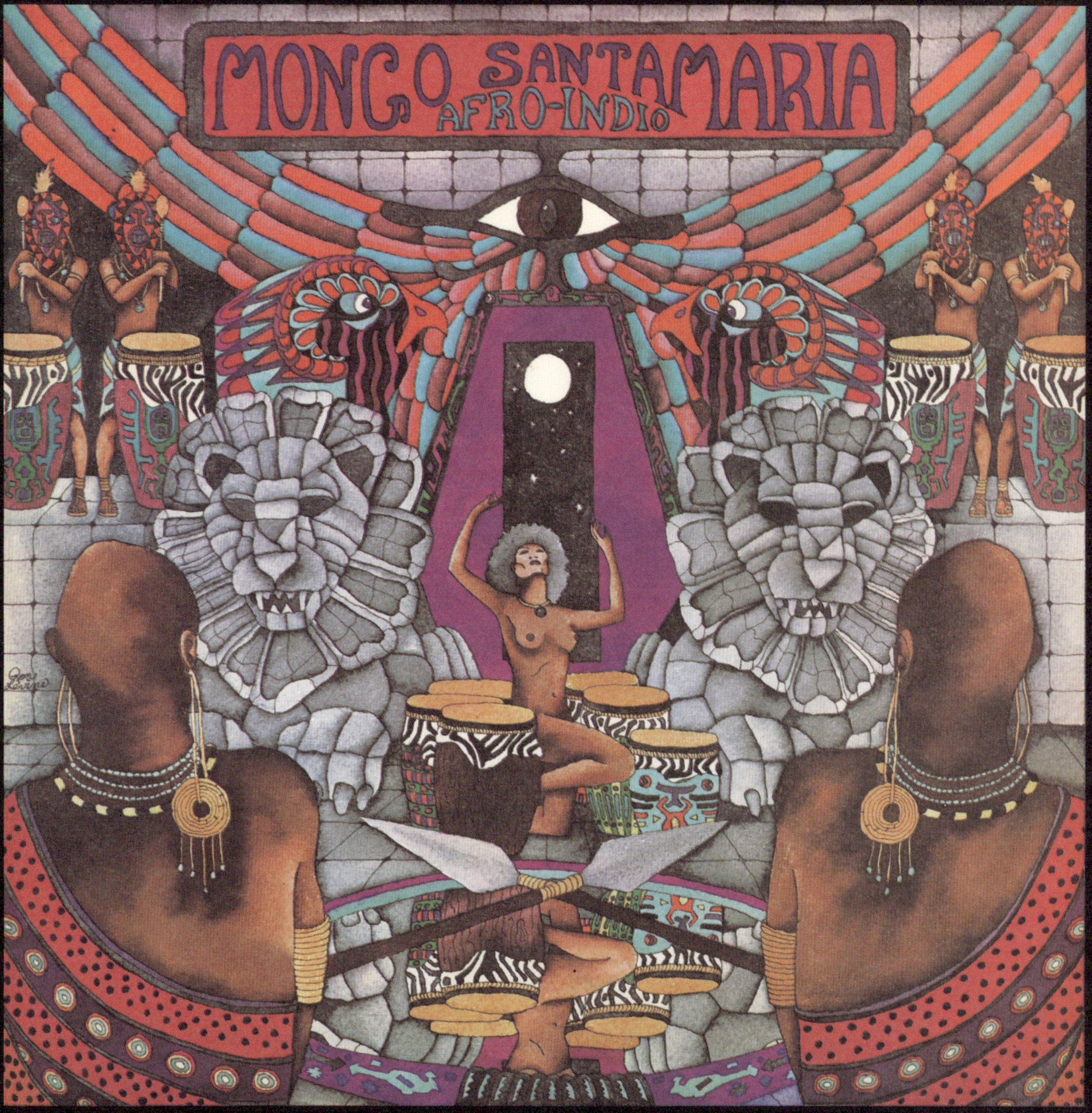

El Chicano Revolución

STEREO KS 3640

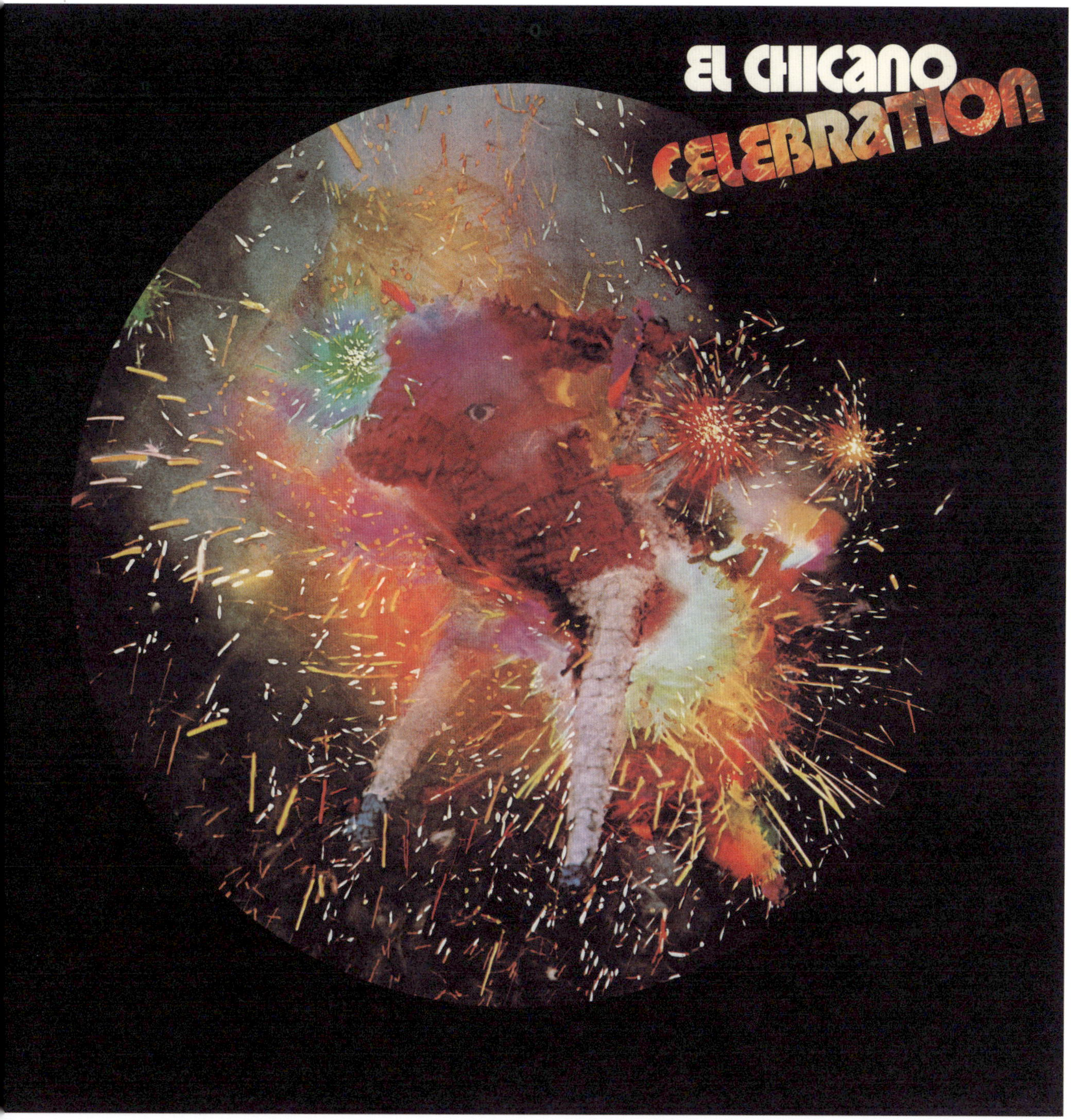
EL CHICANO
CELEBRATION

AZTECA
PYRAMID OF THE MOON

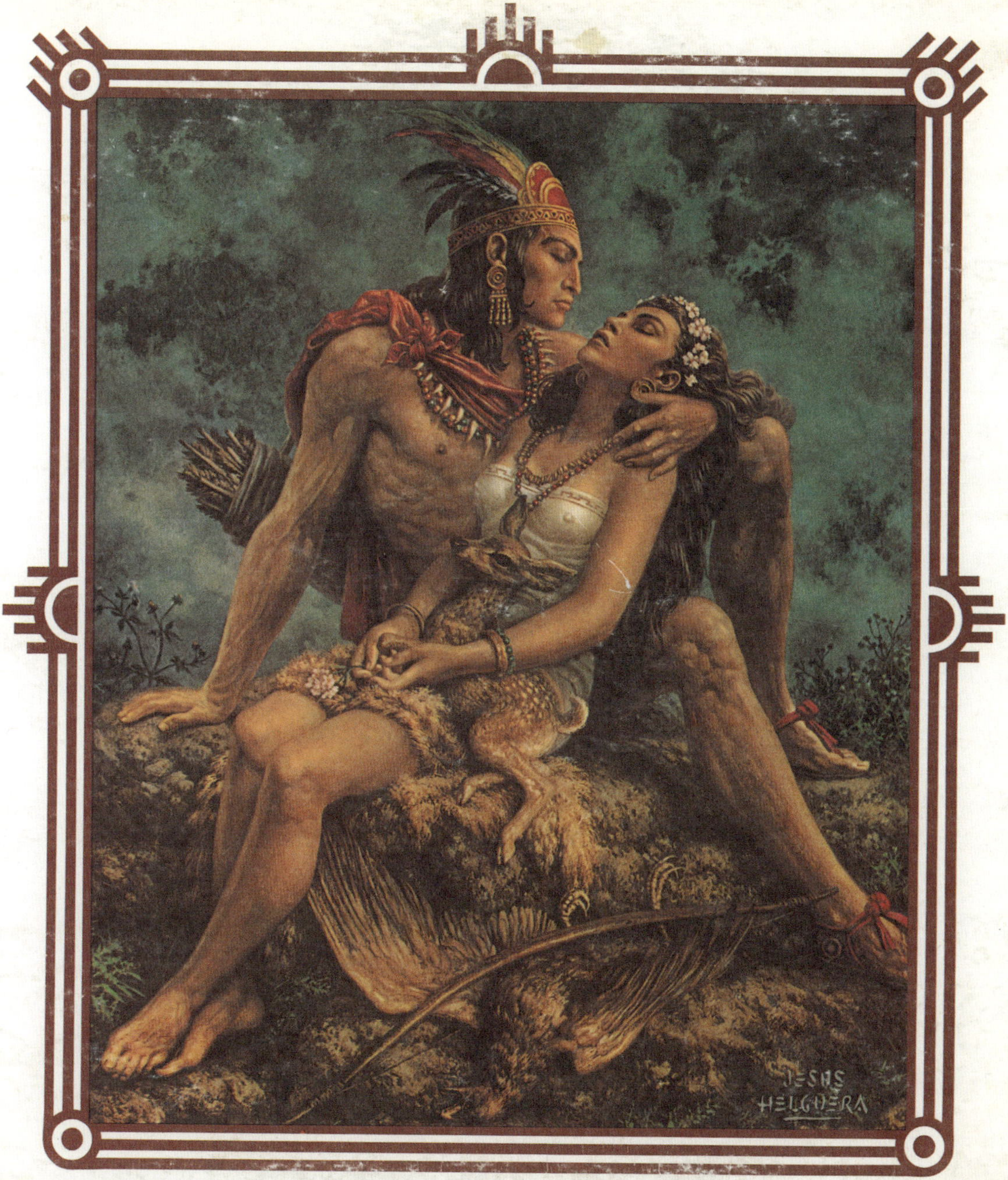
JESUS
HELGUERA

CYS 1312

CAYTRONICS

STEREO
Playable on Monaural Equipment

BWANA

CANDIDO
THOUSAND FINGER MAN

STEREO SS 18066

coco records

CLP 106
COMPATIBLE STEREO

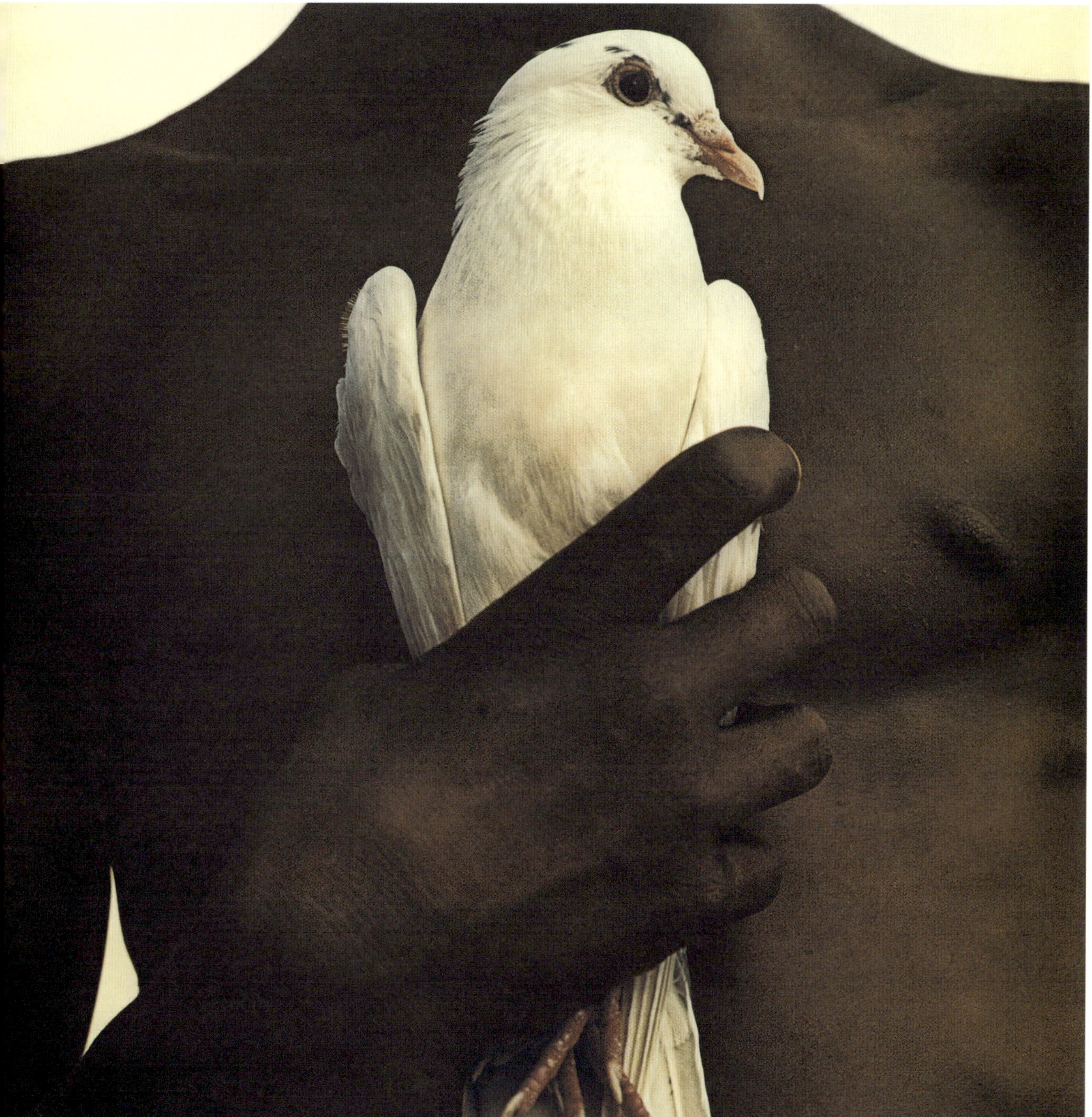

Oh, Meu Brasil

BRAZILIAN MUSIC

1960s–1990s

> To me, *tropicalismo* represented the synthesis between spirituality and Marxism, the people's naive creativity and political militancy. Our album covers represent Brazil itself, all its conflicts and joys, milk and cocoa, naked girls and starving children in the streets, all its richness and misery—Latin America and the third world wailing in front of the gates of the first! —Rogério Duarte

What strikes the viewer upon entering the world of Brazilian album covers, after looking at three decades of Spanish-language music packaging, is just how different and refreshing this aesthetic can be. Yes, there are some similarities: a constant struggle with the idea of the exotic; the use of comic book styles and narrative photography; psychedelia; and portraiture. Yet there is always something peculiarly Brazilian at play, not the least of which are the markers of political, historical, artistic, and cultural difference. The color schemes, dimensions—even the paper stock and printing—are different too.

We begin our journey south with the visual cliché of the Carioca *Carnaval '62*, all posed exuberance and sexy flash. Clara Petraglia's *Brazil*, designed for the U.S. market, is a simple metaphor for the complex duality of her culture, the simple black-and-white division alluding to both African and European ancestry, with the naked (i.e., pure, acoustic, primal, sensuous) singer set squarely in the middle, symbolizing the unique product of this New World commingling: *la música brasileira*. Adjacent is the formally similar cover for the televised songwrtier contest, *3rd Festival da música popular brasileira*, with its guitar eye acting as a sly reference to the TV camera. "MPB" was a new designation, somewhat vague but useful in marketing, much like the term *salsa* in North America.

The U.S. release of João Gilberto's *The Boss of the Bossa Nova* puts the performer in the middle of another eye, the Brazilian flag. With this album, Brazil's new ambassador of song steps into Carmen Miranda's spotlight in the American popular consciousness. The majority of the other albums here are strictly Brazilian releases. Some are for traditional music, while others point to the nation's active musical counterculture, displaying a native commitment to iconoclasm and modernism that complements the futuristic architecture of Oscar Niemeyer's Brasilia or the experiential installation art of Hélio Oiticica.

Contrasting with the bossa king's nationalistic iconography is the decidedly more picaresque demimonde of the samba hustler. Moreira da Silva's *Conversa de Botequim* (Bar Talk) gives visual representation to the scene described in the title song, a wry samba-blues hit penned by Noel Rosa. Da Silva stands in as the *malandro* (swindler), the Brazilian version of a Latino archetype, who sings, "Waiter will you please bring me quickly some fresh coffee and milk and no reheats! Close the door on the right with care 'cause I don't want to be exposed to the sun. Go ask the next customer what the soccer score was and if you keep cleaning the table I won't get up or pay."

From the subdued, cool ambiance of bossa nova we enter into the brave new world of *tropicalismo*. In a sense, tropicália was a home-grown revolution that was poised to take the world by storm, elevating pop culture and challenging the status quo. It was quashed by a brutal imperialism that saw it as a major threat to its hegemony. The following covers are a record of that struggle. Rogério Duarte, the originator of modern Brazilian design and "father of the underground," served as visual interpreter, conceptual advisor, and inspirational rebel role model to the Tropicalist generation.

Tropicália ou panis et circencis (Bread and Circus), from 1968, marks the official start of the movement's musical manifestation, and is considered the first Brazilian concept album. Full of irony and revisionist aesthetics, it was partially inspired by the Beatles' *Sgt. Pepper's Lonely Hearts Club Band* of the previous year, according to Christopher Dunn in his book *Brutality Garden*. The cover, created by designers Rogério Duarte and Antônio Dias with American photographer David Drew Zingg, is a satire of the bourgeois family portrait. Gal Costa and poet-songwriter Torquato Neto appear as a conventional, well-mannered couple. Seated on the bench are composer-arranger Rogério Duprat, daintily holding a chamber pot as if it were a teacup, and Caetano Veloso with a photo of bossa starlet Nara Leão wearing a beach hat. Gilberto Gil sits bohemian-style on the floor in a bathrobe printed with tropical motifs, holding a graduation photo of poet José Carlos Capinan. In the back, rockers Os Mutantes proudly show off their guitars while Tom Zé autobiographically portrays a northeastern migrant holding a characteristic leather satchel. Though at the time intended as a visual allusion to the title track of the album, which parodied the conventions of a traditional bourgeois family, in retrospect it can be seen as a tropical commentary on the *Sgt. Pepper's* cover, with the formerly colonized hungrily raiding the corpse of the colonists. The cover doubly serves as a historic group photo of tropicália's founding "family."

Tom Zé's first solo album of 1968 features the animated facade of a São Paulo street with neonlike signs and cartoon billboards advertising sales, discounts, bingo, toothpaste, gasoline, movies, free newspapers, raffles, strip-tease shows, and even blatant rip-offs like "Take 2, Pay for 3." As Dunn notes, the photo of the singer framed within a television screen appearing under the advertisement "Grande Liquidação: Tom Zé" (Big sale: Tom Zé), is an ironic acknowledgment that as a pop artist he too was a commodity. The album was conceived as a send-up of the culture industry, with its false promises of happiness and abundance for urban consumers. The liner notes begin with the wry comment: "We are an unhappy people bombarded by happiness." This kind of social critique, hyper-awareness, and intellectualism was not so apparent in most Stateside Latin covers of the time.

Gilberto Gil's second solo album of 1968 represented a radical departure from his previous work, and it also bears tropicália's most arresting cover. At first glance he appears to be dressed as an African dictator surrounded by radiating liberation colors of red, gold, and green. Gil is in fact making a deeper, more nuanced statement. In the center photo he is dressed in the official attire of the Brazilian Academy of Letters, a group of forty peer-elected "immortals" consisting at that time entirely of white males. He is wearing bifocals similar to those used by Machado de Assis, the first president of the academy (1897–1908), who was of partial African descent. On the left Gil is brandishing a cane as if to ridicule the real dictators, and on the right he seems to be steering a vehicle without a body, commenting on the disastrous route the elite was taking as the 1960s drew to a close. According to Christopher Dunn, "the image of a black popular musician dressed as an 'immortal' ridiculed the pomposity of 'high' culture and its elitism." It was Duarte and Zingg that helped Gil realize this groundbreaking concept.

In that same year, Duarte and Zingg (joined by artists Liana and Paulo Tavares) helped fellow Bahiano Caetano Veloso present his version of this new music for the release of his first solo album featuring "Tropicália," the song-manifesto that took its name from an influential installation by "anti-artist" Hélio Oiticica. If Veloso's song "allegorized the dilemmas and contradictions of Brazilian modernity," the cover calls to mind something a little more quaint, a Mucha-esque art nouveau Eve in the rain forest. But there is a dark side to this sexy paradise: the serpent climbing Eve's slender pink arm alludes no doubt to the brutality in the Garden of Eden. It is a vision that not only fits in with the tropicalista's critique of the military regime and bourgeois complicity, but also Veloso's preoccupation with retro/kitsch references and Carmen Miranda. Interestingly enough, Duarte's design brings to mind Izzy Sanabria and Walter Velez's concept of "deluxe." Again, this is an appropriation of exoticism in the service of nativism.

The tropicalist movement was a controversial cultural force, and the philosopher/artist Rogério Duarte suffered as a result, though he emerged from his trials with soul intact. Most of his work was destroyed by the military dictatorship which, in the late 1960s, feared a popular youth uprising. The military told the tropicalists and many others to go into exile. Those that did, like Gil and Veloso, were able to come back later, lives relatively intact. Duarte chose to stay, and his association with notorious outlaw bandit Cara de Cavalo (Horse Face) did not help matters. Duarte was subsequently jailed, tortured, and institutionalized in a mental hospital where he was experimented on in lab drug tests. Eventually he was set free and, with his brother Ronaldo (a famous film director), became a drug dealer as the government saw to it there were no other options left to him. The brothers then joined a group of guerrilla fighters in the state of Pernambuco. At some point Duarte escaped this dangerous existence, finding refuge for two years in a Buddhist monastery in the interior, where he learned Sanskrit. He then returned to the slums of Rio, where he joined Cavalo's friends and scraped by for many years living a marginal existence. In the 1980s he became a professor, recently translating the *Bhagavad-Gita* into Portuguese and recording several outstanding music CDs. Last year he was brought out of obscurity and has been celebrated in a book by Narlan Matos.

Though not a Duarte cover, Veloso's sister Maria Bethânia's 1968 live album *Recital na boite barroco* sports another arresting portrait with jungle references. Her insect-covered breasts and El Greco-like hands confront us like Georgia O'Keefe-gone-native. It was a controversial and bizarre cover for its time. Adjacent to her, Jorge Ben serves up another slice of tropical comic book rendering (in a style reminiscent of Ferdinand Léger) that masks some more serious themes. An Afro-Brazilian singer-songwriter from Rio de Janeiro noted for his popular fusions of samba and R&B, Ben's album cover from 1969 features a simple drawing of him surrounded by a psychedelic montage of samba musicians, cartoon female superheroes, tropical plants, and a Brazilian flag. Like some kind of jungle pirate, Ben balances a toucan on his bare muscled shoulder, holding an acoustic guitar emblazoned with the insignia of his favorite soccer team, Flamengo. The broken manacles around his wrist symbolize national and international black struggles. This magical realist portrait mingles the important issues of the day, personal emblems, and symbols of his black Brazilian identity while employing decidedly uptempo pop illustration. This comes as no surprise because, although he was not officially a tropicalista, Ben (or perhaps his cover artist Albery) touched on similar themes. Ben was probably aware of the Neorealist artists (*Neorealismo Carioca*) in Rio who rejected modernist "high" art and looked to popular media such as graphic design, comics, and newspaper photos, experimenting with mass-production and focusing on quotidian urban life. Ben's "colorless" features contrast remarkably with the day-glo rain-forest world surrounding him, reminding one of the arduous road to self-understanding and realization of racial equality. It remains the favorite cover of many fans of MPB.

Gal Costa finishes up the tropicália section with her masterpiece from 1970, *Legal*—a pun not only on her name, but an ironic allusion to the outlaw status bestowed upon most anti-establishment musicians at the time. Though the title does translate literally as "legal," in Brazilian slang it means "cool," or "fine," which only serves to deepen the irony. This cover was designed by Hélio Oiticica, a friend of Andy Warhol and John Cage. It features a portrait of the singer, whose hair bears a collage of various counterculture and pop icons including James Dean, the rebel without a cause, and some of the former tropicalists ("former" because the musical arm of tropicália ended almost as soon as it began). As previously mentioned, Oiticica considered himself to be an anti-artist making "environmental art" that "is much more than macaws and banana trees: it is the consciousness of a non-conditioning to the established structures, therefore, highly revolutionary as a whole. Any conformism, being it intellectual, social or existential, is out of its main idea." Costa and her contemporaries are all represented here by portraits, though not your average glitzy head shots so characteristic of most pop music (salsa included). Rather, the tropicalistas' independent spirit called out for a celebration of self, not hedonistic but full of pride and questioning, a self created by a newly emerging national counter-identity that transformed everything it touched. Oiticica sums it up best: "Our poor universalistic culture, based on the European and North-American ones, should turn to itself, search its own sense, tread on the ground again, make it by hand again, turn to the Blacks and Indians, to the miscegenation."

Brazilian diva Gal Costa, like her friends Os Mutantes (and to a lesser extent Gil and Veloso), had one foot firmly in rock'n'roll, often belting out bluesy songs like Janis Joplin. Her inheritors were a quartet of outlandish rockers whose sacrificed heads show up on dinner plates. Secos & Molhados burst on the scene in an atmosphere of oppression and censorship, and their last-supper offering, like their live performances, no doubt shocked and titillated. "The Dry and the Wet" was a pun on the idiomatic Brazilian expression for "general store." According to author Claus Schreiner in his book *Música Brasileira*, their slogan was "freedom in every respect." Their music, like that of the tropicalists, often had an "everything but the kitchen sink" mentality to it. They sold 500,000 copies of their debut album in 1973 (a figure in Brazil on par with the Beatles), won top album cover ratings in the polls, and disappeared a year later. Lead singer Ney Matogrosso was known as "Brazil's Alice Cooper." The band combined modern and traditional elements, used verse by famous poets for their lyrics, and affected a decidedly "glam" presence on stage. Makeup, feathers, and bandannas call to mind both Kiss and *Beggar's Banquet*-era Stones.

Hot on the heels of the fantasmagorical *Secos & Molhados* LP, the oft celebrated magical realism of South America is evident in the covers of Baden Powell, Deodato, and João Bosco. Glaugo Rodrigues created Bosco's *Caça a raposa* jacket painting, appropriating stock *carioca* imagery but recombining it in an ironic way. Born in 1922, he was already an established painter in the 1960s, and he participated in the *Nova Objetividade* (New Objectivist) show of 1967. For the most part, objectivists like Rodrigues and Oiticica sought to create environments that emphasized practice or participation as opposed to the creation of objects for passive consumption. Rodrigues later painted important national allegories in the tropicalist vein. His *Primeira Missa* (1971) touches on notions of race, history, and the exotic.

This chapter has its own folkloric/religious section, with fine examples of African-inspired cover art. As Robert Farris Thompson explains, artist Nilo Jorge's iconography on Luiz da Muriçoca's live album *Cânticos de terreiro* of 1971 illustrates how the world was prepared for the great Afro-Atlantic religions via LPs that had a lot of cultural information on them. The main figure is Exú (*orixa*, or deity of the crossroads), formed and worshiped in a modernized Bahian way; the drums are the engine for the ritual expressions of *Candomblé* (a predominantly Yoruba-based system of worship); the other mystical symbols, serpent and trident, are from *Candomblé* and *Macumba*, a predominantly Kongo-based system of worship. Like so many modes of New World expression and identity, there is a mix of once disparate cultures, here the black traditions of Rio and Bahia. These symbols, as well as the title, identify the songs as coming from the *terreiro*, the place of worship. The simplicity and homemade quality of the art and layout clue the viewer in to the music's folk roots. The *Canto negro* album shares a similar "afro" aesthetic and was painted by samba troupe Ilê Aiyê's costume designer, J. Cunha.

What draws the viewer in to the *Candomblé* album cover is the feeling that the cover privileges the voyeuristic gaze, allowing the possessor of the LP access one might not have otherwise. According to Thompson, who has been involved in the ceremony depicted, the cover photo shows that we are being exposed to one of the deepest of the religion's secrets. He explains: "when one takes the feather of *ashé* [the divine spark, flash of the spirit] and enters under Exú's protection, as that power radiates through the entranced initiate, she breaks out into the skin of a leopard, the most royal of all animals, powerful lithe hunter, something never shown on an LP cover before." The word *Candomblé* means "all that is blackened is important."

The folkloric section ends with a startling cover by Carol Wald for the American jazz flautist Paul Horn's intriguing *Altura do Sol* (*High Sun*), documenting an Anglo's encounter with Brazil. The viewer is accosted by a photo montage showing that behind the mask of the "Other" we see ourselves, the blond hair blazing like the sun in the title. Horn declares in the notes that "the band was cookin'" and with pieces like "Dança das cabecas (Head Dance)" and "Quarup (Worship Ceremony)," the tribalistic music and masquerade art are a perfect match.

The chapter concludes with a quartet of covers that focus the gaze on the body, up close and personal (though note that no male body parts are scrutinized). Gal Costa "goes native" (the exotic again) for her 1973 recording *Índia*, reiterating tropicalist desires for employing an anti-intellectual process that sought to create, in the words of Oiticica, "the miscegenation myth.... The creation of an authentic Brazilian culture, distinctive and strong, at least expressive, demands that the damned European and North-American heritage be absorbed, in a cannibalistic way, by the Black and Indian heritages of our land, which are, in fact, the only significant ones because most of the Brazilian art products are hybrid, intellectualized to the maximum, with no individual meaning." Despite these idealistic aims, Brazil (like the U.S. in relation to its Latino population) remains a tableau of irreconcilable difference, and the exploitative nature of Costa's semi-nude masquerading *caboclo*-style on the front and back cover only supports this (*caboclo* is a term that denotes masquerading as an Indian). A journalist, on seeing Gal Costa live in 1973, commented: "The audience was below the level of the stage and saw clearly the image shown on the LP cover. But under the grass skirt there was no biquini [sic]!"

From the crotch we move to the bottom, this one being stung by an oversized, Amazonian mosquito in Jorge Mautner's *Antimaldito*. The title translates as "anti-damned," though what that means in terms of the cover is up for interpretation. Rogério Duarte told this author: "Well, well yes it was my idea—but what it means—I know very well: dive into the ocean and see how the fishes are!!" Perhaps going native can be painful, especially if the fishes are piranhas; we enter the jungle but may never make it out alive. This author's reaction upon stumbling on this artwork was similar to the man pictured.

We progress naturally from Mautner's deluxe-ly poor taste posterior to the ultimate pair of covers, coming full circle back to the gaze with a suite of eyes. On the left, the heavy metal album *Clara crocodilo,* with its title written in oozing blood, stares balefully back at us from the deepest savage mangrove swamps of the Rio Amazonas. Yet nothing can prepare one for the perverse act of subversion dreamed up by Brazil's true iconoclast, Tom Zé, on his 1973 album inspired by

Brazilian concrete poetry, *Todos os olhos* (All of the Eyes). What first appears to be a closeup of a planet in space or a glass eye actually turns out to be a photo of a green marble resting gently in a woman's rear end, shot in soft focus. This cover was literally an in-your-face gesture to the censors during the most repressive phase of military rule. Zé recounted many years later: "My friends had fun telling me 'I saw that anus in the middle of the Plaza of the Republic!' Sometimes people suspected, but we always denied it. We talked about how Brazil was an anus at that time, it was the face of Brazil. I never met the girl personally. Today I encourage her, even if she has grandchildren, to come forward. The commercial exhibition of her anus, which could be morally doubtful, today is even patriotic."

RCA VICTOR
BBL-1162
MÚSICA POPULAR
A VOZ DO DONO
New Orthophonic High Fidelity Recording
CARNAVAL
RCA
62

WF 12024

Westminster HI-FI

BRAZIL

Photo: Maria Martel

3º festival da música popular brasileira

R 765.014 L

PHILIPS

realização da **tv record** de são paulo

VOLUME 1

℗ 1967

série De Luxe

PHILIPS

THE BOSS OF THE BOSSA NOVA
JOÃO GILBERTO

STEREO

8070 ATLANTIC

IPM 30196
Imperial
CONVERSA DE BOTEQUIM
CONTA
ESPORTES
moreira da silva

TROPICALIA

OU PANIS ET CIRCENCIS

R 765.040

PHILIPS
série De Luxe

PHILIPS
℗ 1968

especial
rozenblit
LP 50.010
LAY-OUT officina
GRANDE LIQUIDAÇÃO
TOM·ZÉ
PONHA
UM TIG
NOSEU
NÔVO
CREME DENTAL!
AH!!
VOCÊ GANHA 10 MILHÕES E 50 VOLKS
SEM SORTEIO !!!
SÓ tal tem qual
BINGO
HOJE · 32ª
EVE 2
AGUE 3
EXTRA
RÁTIS
TOM·ZÉ
SATORU·68

R 765.024 L

Rogerio Duarte + Antonio Dias + David Drew Zingg

GILBERTO GIL

CAETANO VELOSO
PHILIPS
R 765. 026 L
série
De Luxe
PHILIPS
© 1967

MOFB 3545

ODEON

℗1968

ALTA FIDELIDADE

MARIA BETHÂNIA

RECITAL NA BOITE BARROCO

GRAVADO AO VIVO

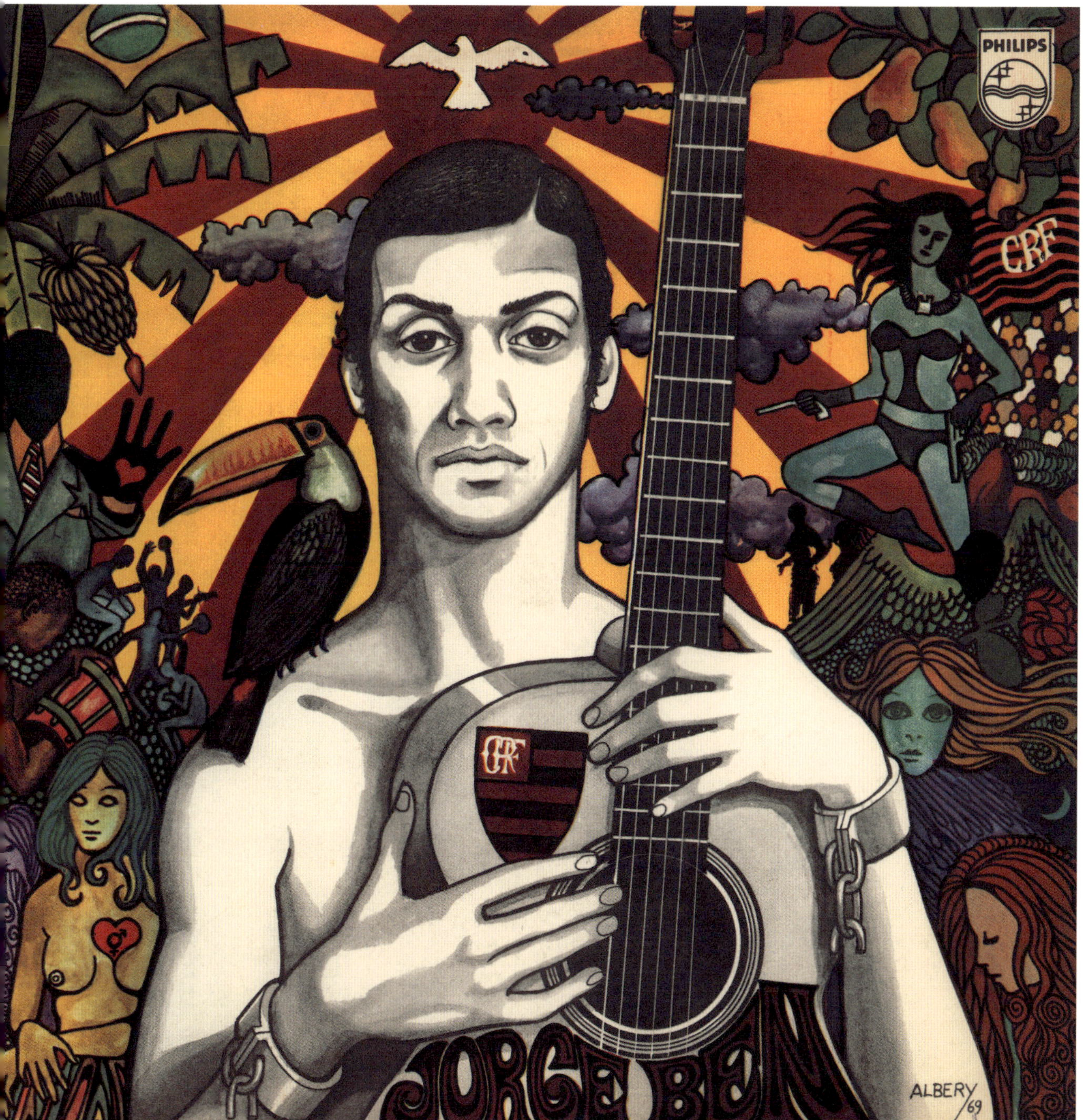
PHILIPS
CRF
CRF
JORGE BEN
ALBERY/69

LEGAL

Secret Oyster

Baden Powell
Images on Guitar

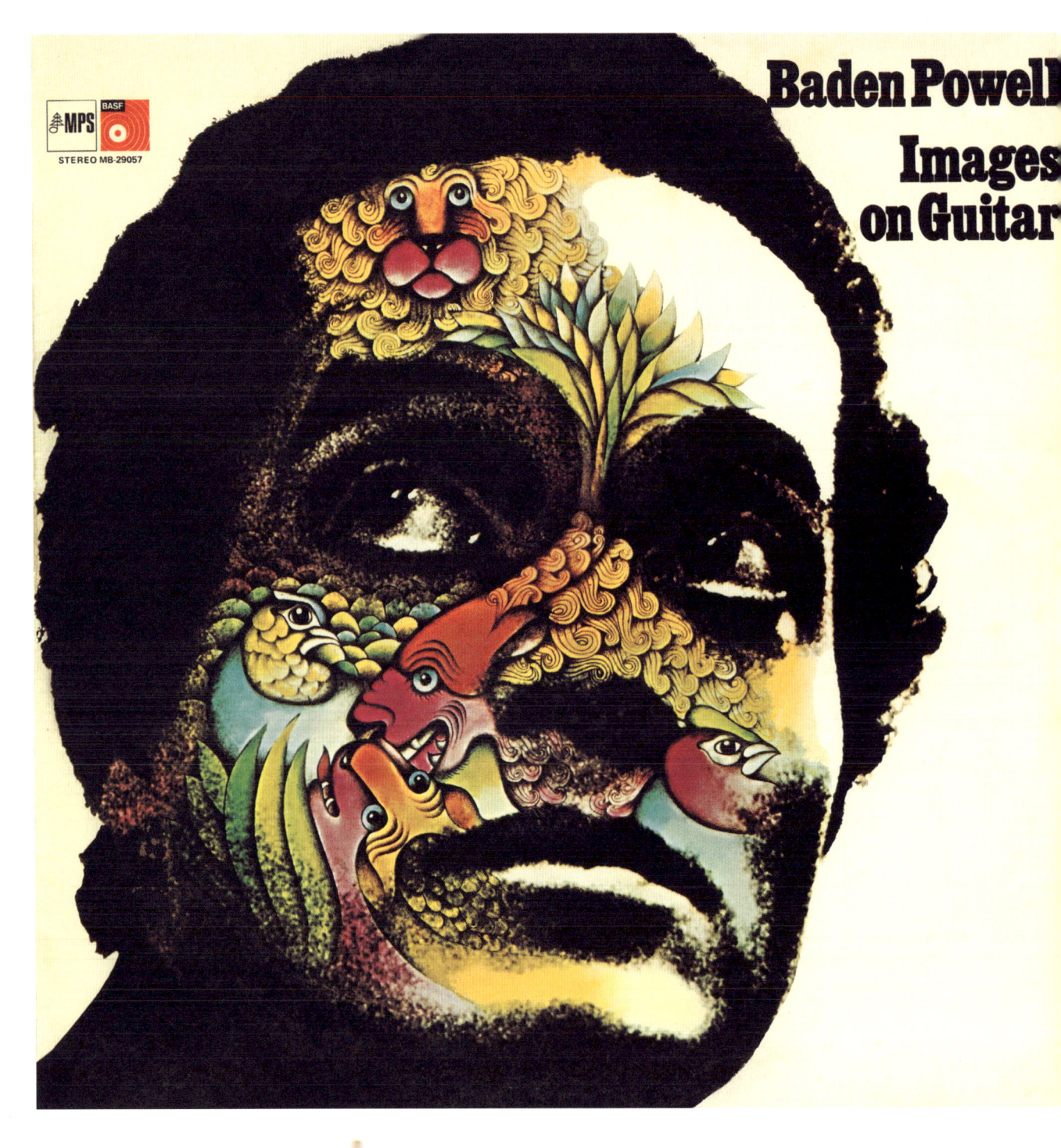

MPS BASF
STEREO MB-29057

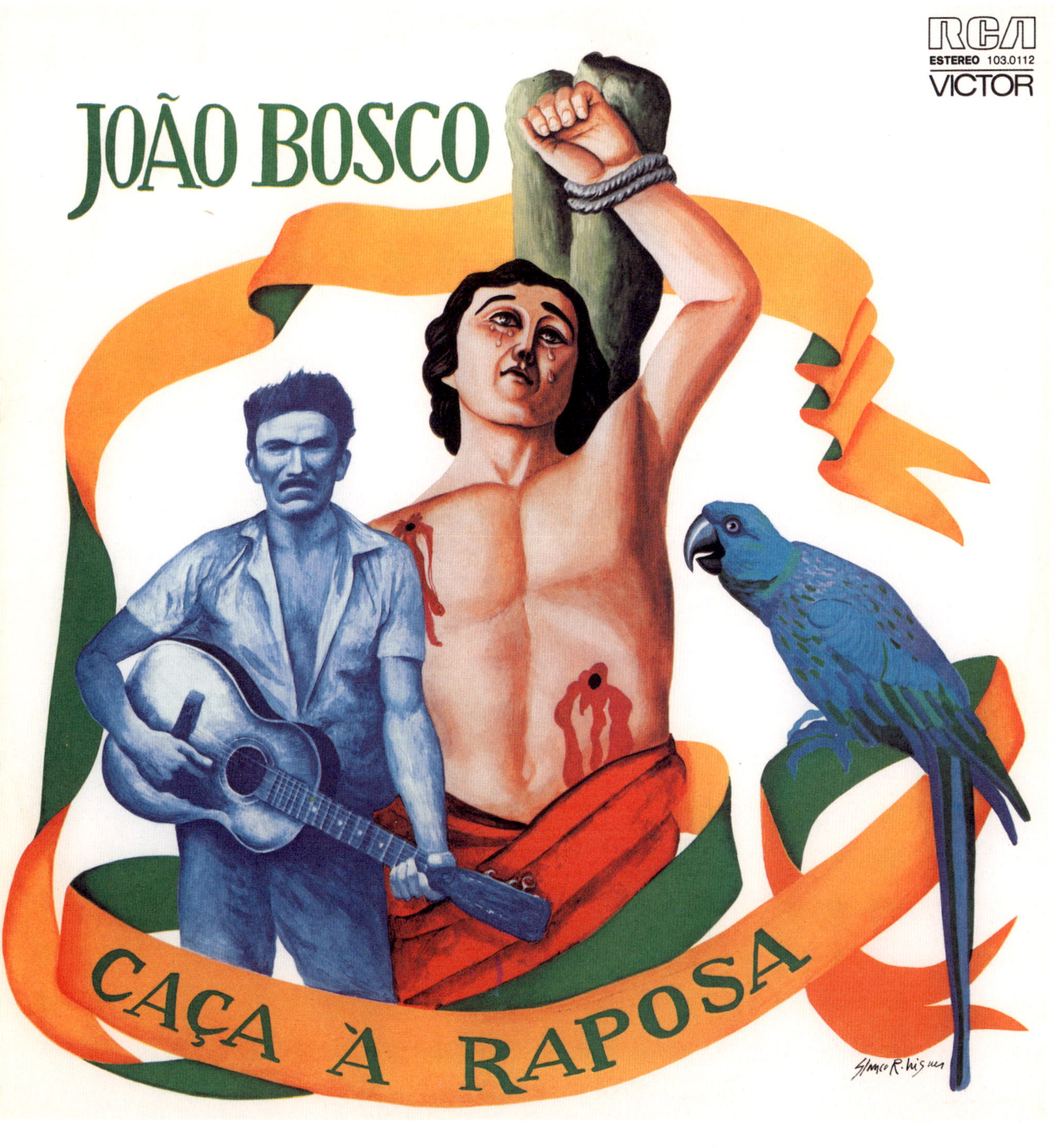
RCA
ESTEREO 103.0112
VICTOR
JOÃO BOSCO
CAÇA À RAPOSA

CÂNTICOS DE TERREIRO
LUIZ DA MURIÇOCA

ILÊ AIYÊ

CANTO NEGRO

CANDOMBLÉ

Paul Horn

Altura Do Sol
(High Sun)

ÍNDIA

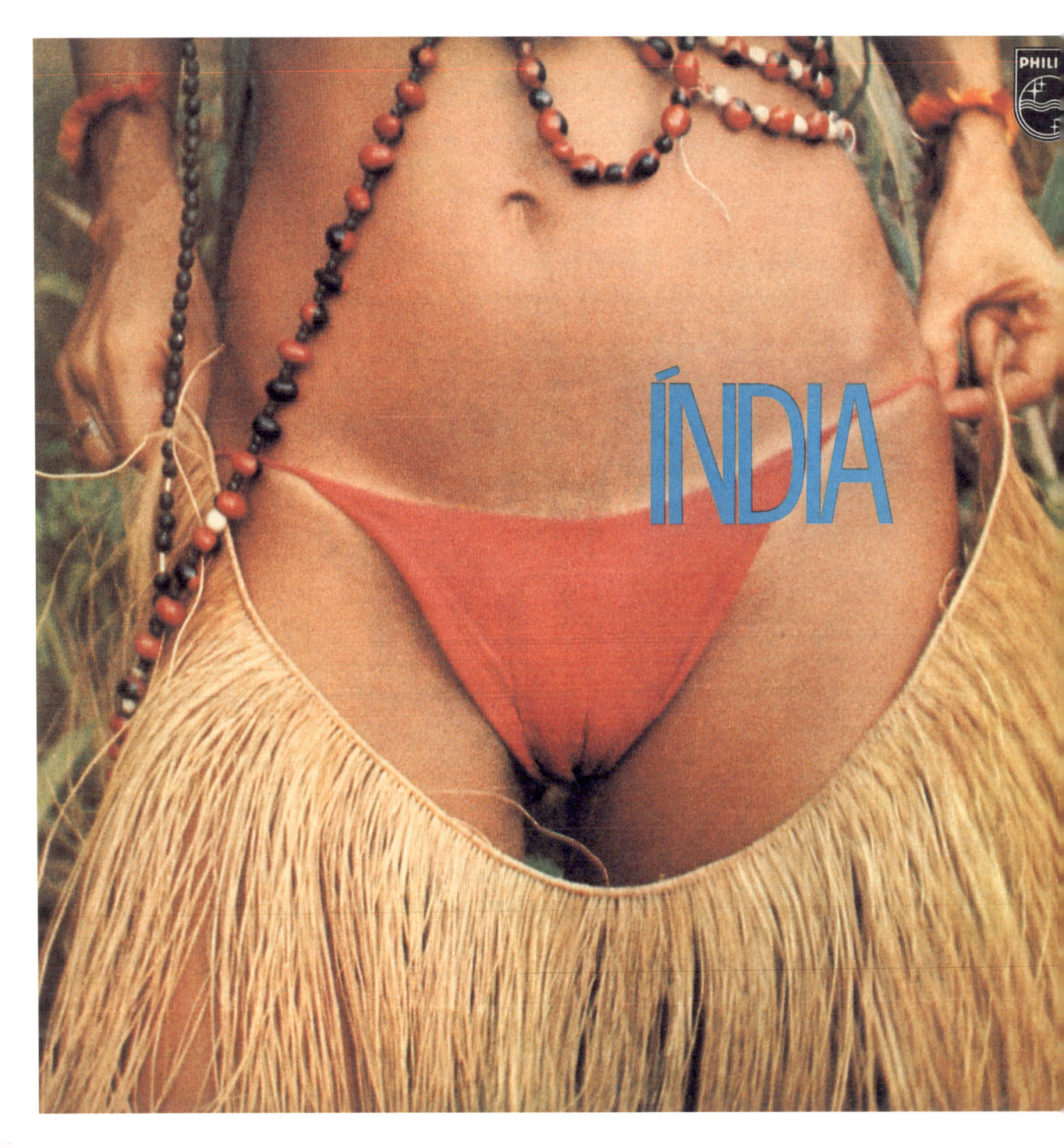

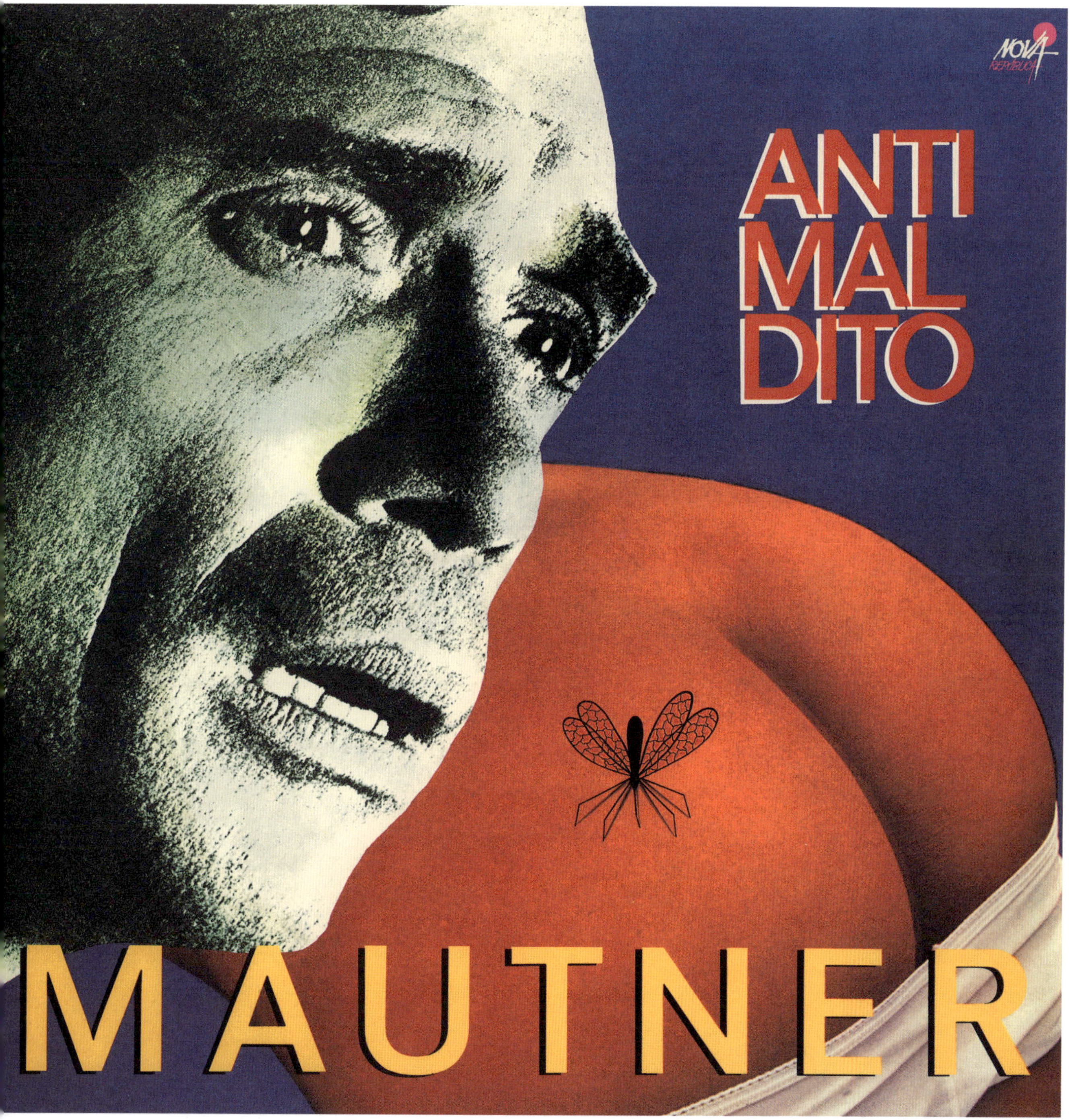
NOVA REPUBLICA
ANTI
MAL
DITO
MAUTNER

CLARA CROCODILE

TOMZÉTODOSOSOLHOS

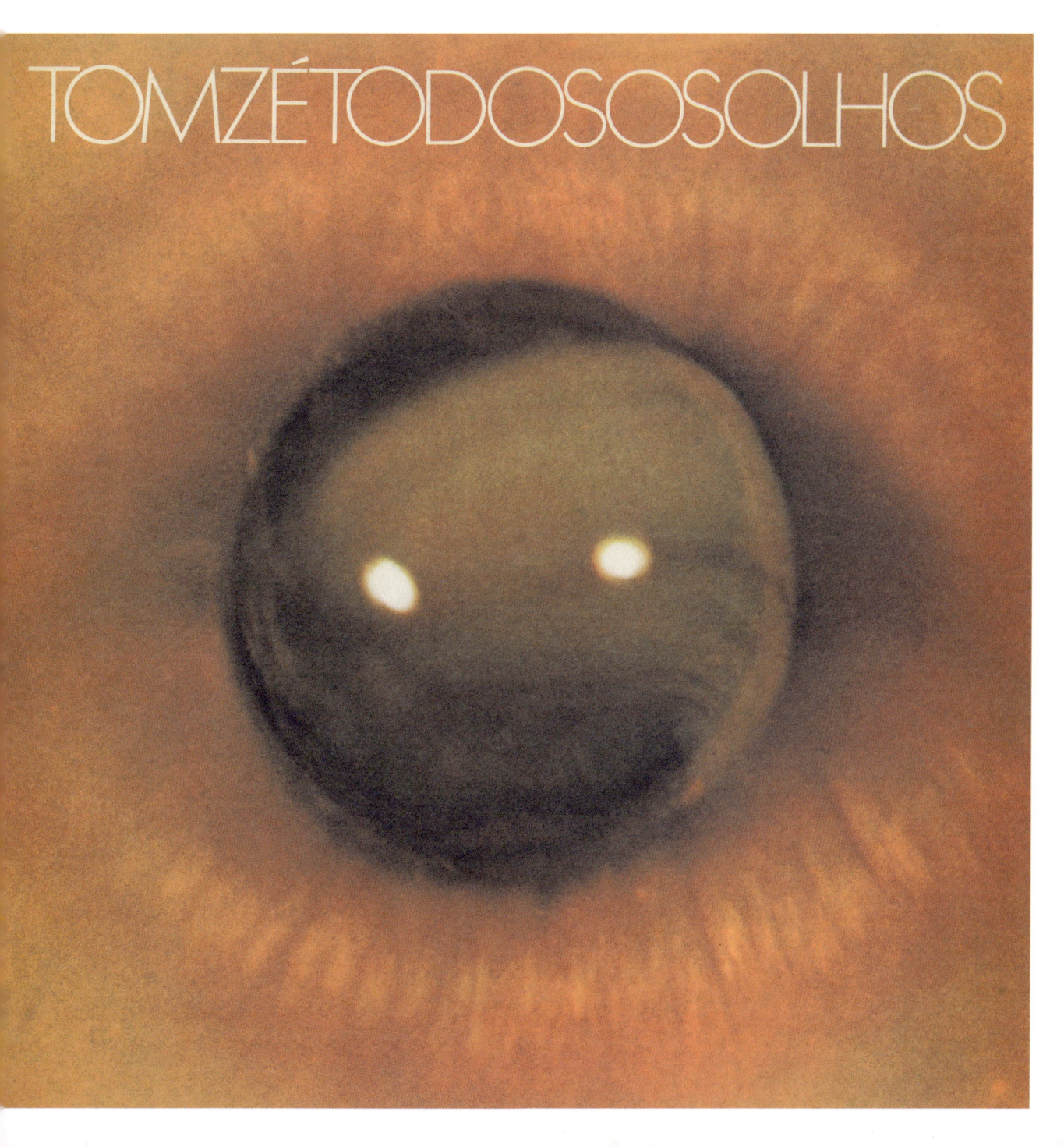

Barrio Nuevo

CONTEMPORARY

LATIN MUSIC

If some of the older designers were growing tired of the demands and limitations of the salsa machine, and the traditional 12-inch format hindered creativity, the digital revolution would make available a whole new arsenal of tools and usher in a fresh crop of graphic artists. Inevitably, there was conflict. Ely Besalel: "Toward the late 1980s and early 1990s, the Latin companies I worked for fell apart, people I knew weren't around anymore, and when things went digital...they didn't give a damn about the quality any more. I was even being told to produce covers that *looked* like they had been done in a computer, to show they were technology-oriented." In fact, some of the most interesting work was coming from abroad.

It is often the British and Japanese who adopt American genres that are forgotten, ignored, or taken for granted on their home turf. UK import *Barrio Nuevo* has a simple cover that is reminiscent of the best of Tico or Fania. The layout impacts through its use of a bold newsprint font, purposefully low-budget production values, and an arresting black-and-white snapshot of Latino youth—though the markers of the past are now used to signify retro beats for the vinyl junkie generation. Many current Latin reissues reference old-school design aesthetics, sampling past icons the way hip hop DJs sample the music.

From its inception, hip hop was embraced by the Latino community; *East Side Story* by Kid Frost is a prime example. The cover follows the titles of Frost's raps and proclaims a story central to urban Mexican-American identity: a *vato loco* (hood) on the run, his lowrider showering sparks and dollars while LAPD choppers chase overhead. The character is a cousin to Willie Colón's *el malo* and da Silva's *malandro*, another example of the archetypal street tough. The "O" in the title "Kid Frost" is reminiscent of the gun sight in the rap group Public Enemy's logo, symbolizing both the gangbanger's weapon of choice and the ever-present eye of the police. The lettering of "East Side Story" purposefully ties in with Broadway's *West Side Story* poster layout, and the illustration by a graffiti artist named Cartoon looks like a Mexican mural gone hip hop. The apparent appropriation of black idioms (yet again) is actually something of a misconception here, thanks to the marketing of rap as an exclusively African-American musical style with an Afrocentric message. As old school Puerto Rican hip hop DJ Charlie Chase put it succinctly in Juan Flores' *From Bomba to Hip-Hop*: "What you talking about, a Black thing man? I was part of the Cold Crush Brothers, man. We opened doors for you guys...it's a street thing. I liked it because it came from the street and I'm from the street....to me, rap is colorblind, that's that!" Though Nuyorican hip hoppers might have been on the street all along, they did not play up their Latino identities until acts like Latin Empire and Mellow Man Ace realized the use of ethnic imagery and the "Latin lingo" in raps were essential to get these stories over to their audience.

Meanwhile, Rubén Blades and Seis del Solar's *Escenas* (*Scenes*) presented the updated East Coast barrio of 1985. Here we have a New York street scene looking much the same as it did during salsa's golden era, but this time the high production values and noir touches suggest a still from a movie set—no doubt because of Blades' experiences acting in films like *Crossover Dreams* and *The Last Fight*. One band member cleans his nails with a *navaja* (knife) on a stoop, echoing Blades' 1978 hit (with Willie Colón) "Pedro Navaja," a picaresque tale of a Puerto Rican Mack the Knife who shows up in *Escenas* for a cameo tune. A stuffed cat, frozen band members, and a business-suited pedestrian add to the stiff artificiality. In the rose-tinted window, an older mother watches the boys outside, while Rubén looks up to see a dove flying away overhead. The first song on the album tells of a mother afraid of the dark ever since the father left home, who "believes that the heart dues can never be paid in full." Blades is a storyteller, and each figure on the cover is a character in this urban novella.

Flashback to Blades's first Elektra release, the award-winning precursor to *Escenas*, 1984's *Buscando América*. For this cover, Blades and photographer Ricardo Betancourt take us back in time before the arrival of Latinos in the barrio to an even more primal, dramatic scene. A colonial/tropical sky illuminated with the red glow of dawn forms a gripping backdrop, the blue faces of the band members staring up full of hope and fear, recalling images of border crossings in the night, arrival on Ellis Island early in the morning, or perhaps even religious visions of the seventeenth century. Blades saw a picture of prehistoric cavemen in a tableau, and it struck him as appropriate to symbolize "all the conflict in Central America at the time, the red being war, the blue being peace. People always look somewhere else for answers to their pain." An album filled with humanitarian themes, Blades' title song echoed the cover: "I am searching for America, and I fear I won't find it. Its traces have become lost amongst the darkness. I'm calling for America but it can't answer me. Those afraid of truth have made her disappear." The nostalgic landscape of memory and the loss of loves past are symbolized by the empty house and palm tree on the horizon, echoed in the evocative old ballad "Todos Vuelven," in which everyone returns to the land where they were born and a mysterious voice tells us that "the love of this earth is sacred, that the absence of yesterdays is sad." The church's silhouette to the right of the figures, as well as being a marker of faith and the colonial heritage, resonates with the bell tolling for Padre Antonio and the altar boy, Andrés, in the last song on the album. Padre Antonio, who came to the jungle searching for new promises, preaches love and condemns violence, and for this he and his altar boy are murdered in cold blood. "It's the conflict between the terrestrial and the spiritual," says Blades. The bells ring in the church tower for those who have fallen.

Though Ron Levine was phasing himself out of the album cover business in the mid-1980s, he did execute paintings for Johnny Pacheco, the Fania All-Stars, Larry

Harlow, Sonora Ponceña, and Héctor Lavoe. Levine's painting for Lavoe's *El Sabio* (The Wiseman), has a pleasantly expository quality that lends itself to the idea of the math teacher giving lessons, a reference to Lavoe's instrumental role as the voice of salsa. As Levine explains: "Jerry said 'I want Hector as a teacher.' So I used my friend Pierre, who was a linguist and a poet, as the model. It was very simple and stark, but I spent a lot of time on it. I used the blackboard again on the back to list the credits. The mathematical formula on the front changed to read '= Salsa' on the back. Take all these equations, try to explain it, and it just comes up one word. You can't really teach that stuff. I just wanted to challenge myself . . . and also make the musical artist look great." Ironically, if Lavoe's career teaches us anything, it is that great talent can be a burden as well as a gift, and that when the gifted cannot handle their special talents, the equation can become unbalanced, with dire consequences. And an unintended metaphor of the album's imagery suggested that salsa had been reduced to a commercial formula.

Positioning a Latino as a professor, a step up from all those gangsters and superheroes, had not been done before. Another portrait of Latinos in white collar roles, though with a humorous veneer, is Cuban supergroup Los Van Van's *El negro no tiene na*, with the hit tune of the same name depicted on the cover. In the song, handsome vocalist, dancer, and percussionist Pedrito Calvo denies charges he had contracted a disease from one of his many amorous exploits (remember this is the 1980s, a time of dangerous denial about the impact of AIDS) as he is attended to by two lighter-skinned doctors. The layout is thoroughly modern, in the spirit of the New Wave covers of the time and decidedly un-Fania.

Also from Cuba, Dan Den take their onomatopoeic name from the sound of the cowbell in the carnival of Bejucal, hometown of bandleader Juan-Carlos Alfonso. *Siempre hay un hojo que te ve* (There Is Always an Eye Watching You) is one of the highlights of this book. Though the title song is ostensibly a smooth, trombone-led romantic salsa ballad about people "checking each other out," below the surface there is a deeper meaning, an allusion to state surveillance and control through censorship, patronage, and the local Committee for the Defence of the Revolution, a notorious neighborhood block watch association. The use of black and white illustration on matte paper stock may be due to shortages in materials, but by the 1990s the U.S. blockade and the dissolution of the USSR had fostered a culture in which Cubans were increasingly adept at making do with less, and at least here the product is even stronger for it.

Another version of the gaze, this time obscured by sunglasses, comes from *alternativa* group Yerba Buena. *President Alien* confronts us with the view of the outsider while turning on its head the contradictory notion of "resident alien" as a divisive form of Latino identity. The cover recalls Larry Harlow's *Heavy Smokin'*, made some forty years earlier, a vision of hipster cool. Here, the startling artificial idyll reflected in Andrés Levin's aviators shows us only what we want to see. He seems to ask: how can we think of Latinos, especially those with indigenous blood, as illegal aliens in their own land?

Moving into real alien territory, Ron Levine's controversial *Star Wars*-inspired album painting for Sonora Ponceña presages the Luaka Bop release of New York's techno-ska group King Changó. Band leader/graphic designer Andrés "Blanquitoman" Blanco deftly mixes an ancient Yoruba name-check with Aztec echoes, Mexican pop culture, and high-tech combat robotics that call to mind some twisted Atari action game. The main figure on the cover of *Return of El Santo* refers to the legendary Mexican pro wrestler El Santo, seen here in his patented *diablo* costume. (Blanco also designed the aggressive logo for the NBA's Toronto Raptors).

Africando and Orishas both represent Afro-Cuban-based music coming full circle. On the one hand, the shield-like/tribal marking device bearing salsa group Africando's name points to their African identity; on the other, Orisha's hand-drawn *Emigrante* (Emigrant) would never be confused with typically slick contemporary commercial Latin CD design in that it references West Coast psychedelic rock posters and international fantasy/graphic novel aesthetics to signal its alternative nature, though the roosters, cigars, *caimânes* (alligators) and jungle goddesses are "ethnic" enough to be construed as somewhere between African and Caribbean. Framed in the center in black and white, the poses of rappers Yotuel, Roldán, and Ruzzo are strictly b-boy hip hop in attitude, as opposed to Africando's classically suited trio. What works in pairing the two covers is their circular symmetry.

The next four plates employ nostalgic imagery traditionally associated with Latino identity: Grupo Niche, who play classic retro *salsa dura*, revive the dandy Latin Lover, while Conjunto Céspedes' *Flores* flirts with colorful 1950s tropical folkisms.

Nuyorican Soul and *Good Morning Aztlán* go deeper. Both Masters at Work and Los Lobos are concerned as much with roots and community as they are with cutting edge technology or experimental music, and while they are constantly looking ahead to new fusions and directions, one foot always stays firmly planted *en la madre tierra*, in this case the Motherland being Nu Yorica and Aztlán, respectively, semi-mythologized places of origin on opposite coasts. Both feature sunrise symbolism (the promise of a new day), conjure up classic Latin product design loaded with multiple signifiers (cigar boxes from the Caribbean and fruit labels from Mexi/Cali), and sneak contemporary references in to signal that though these projects are a look back, they are also a look forward, being contemporary and vital, like the best music of the people. *Aztlán* translates from the Nahuatl as "near the crane," the place of origin for the Aztecs, and indeed the disk inside features the noble bird in a petroglyph; on the back of *Good Morning Aztlán*, we see a green and white highway sign pointing to Aztlán somewhere down the L.A. freeway. The front shows us that ancient Aztlán is really in the heart and mind of the people, anywhere they want it to be, even the bungalos and basketball courts of East L.A. Art director and multi-instrumentalist band member Louie Pérez worked with Tornado Design, the team responsible for Los Lobos' phenomenally attractive four CD box set retrospective *El Cancionero (Más y Más)*, which also features an intriguingly anachronistic mix of 1930s Mexican film poster stylings and contemporary *vato* homeboy imagery that recalls the Kid Frost cover. *Nuyorican Soul*, "Little" Louie Vega and Kenny "Dope" Gonzalez's homage to their disco and salsa roots, allowed them to rework and create new tunes with old heroes. The island of Manhattan is not known for its palm trees, beaches, or cigar *fábricas*, but this album is about freedom of expression, where the divas smoke fat stogies and dance music can indeed be all things to all people.

We serve up the final course in this look at fifty years of Latin cover art with a *postre* (dessert) of the dreaded "cult of personality" portrait. But if we are talking roots and good taste, there is nothing deluxe about the voice of *Buena Vista*, Don Ibrahim Ferrer. His dignity and perseverance shine through the tinted gaze of Western consumers' cultural imperialism. We end with the unforgettable diva *de pura madre* of Latin music, Celia Cruz, one deluxe woman who knew how to cook!

Barrio Nuevo

LATIN FUNK · LATIN ROCK · LATIN DISCO · LATIN SOUL

KID FROST
EAST SIDE STORY
FROST
PARENTAL ADVISORY EXPLICIT LYRICS

Rubén Blades
y Seis del Solar

Rubén Blades y Seis del Solar

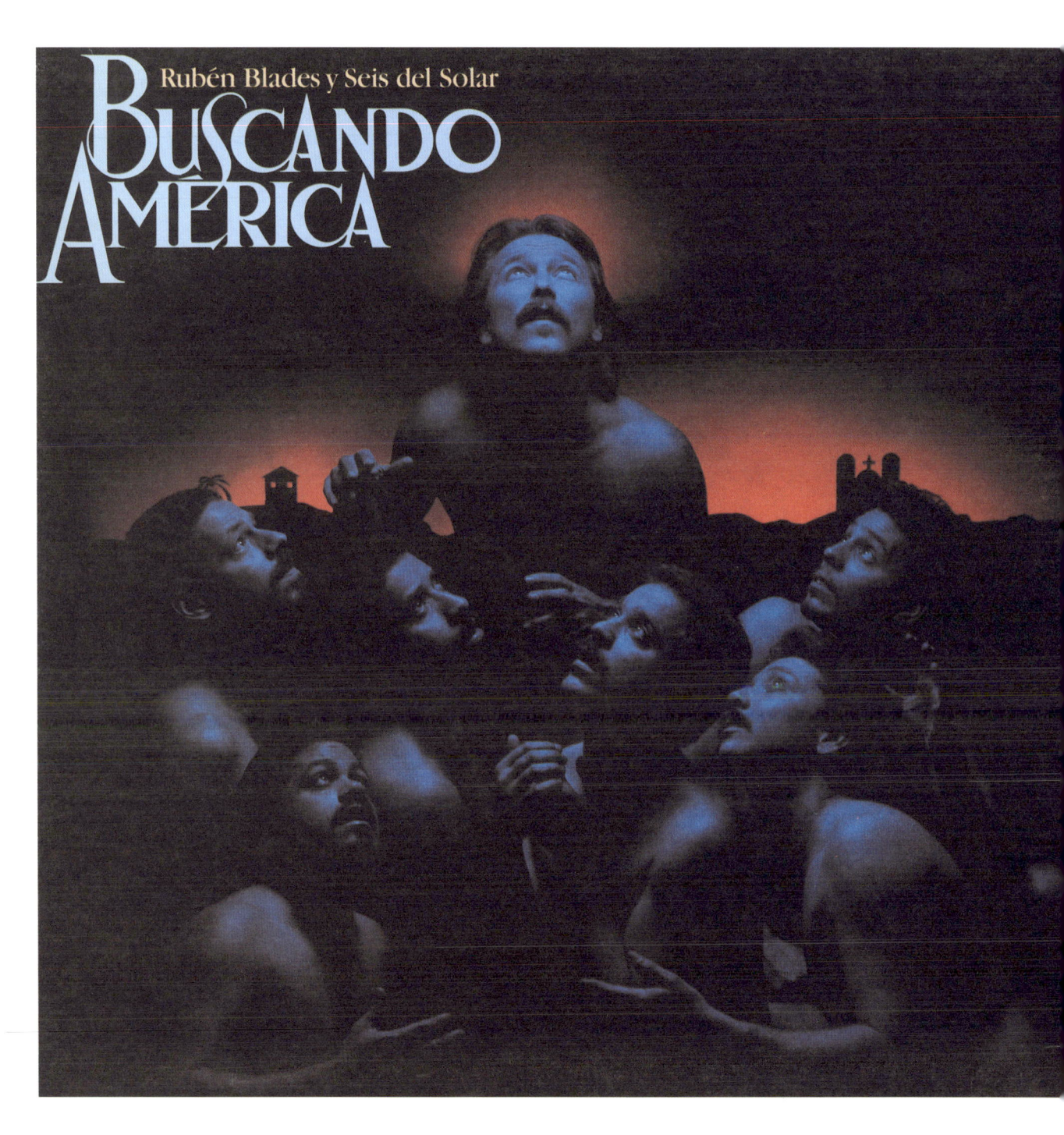

Buscando América

YOMO TORO

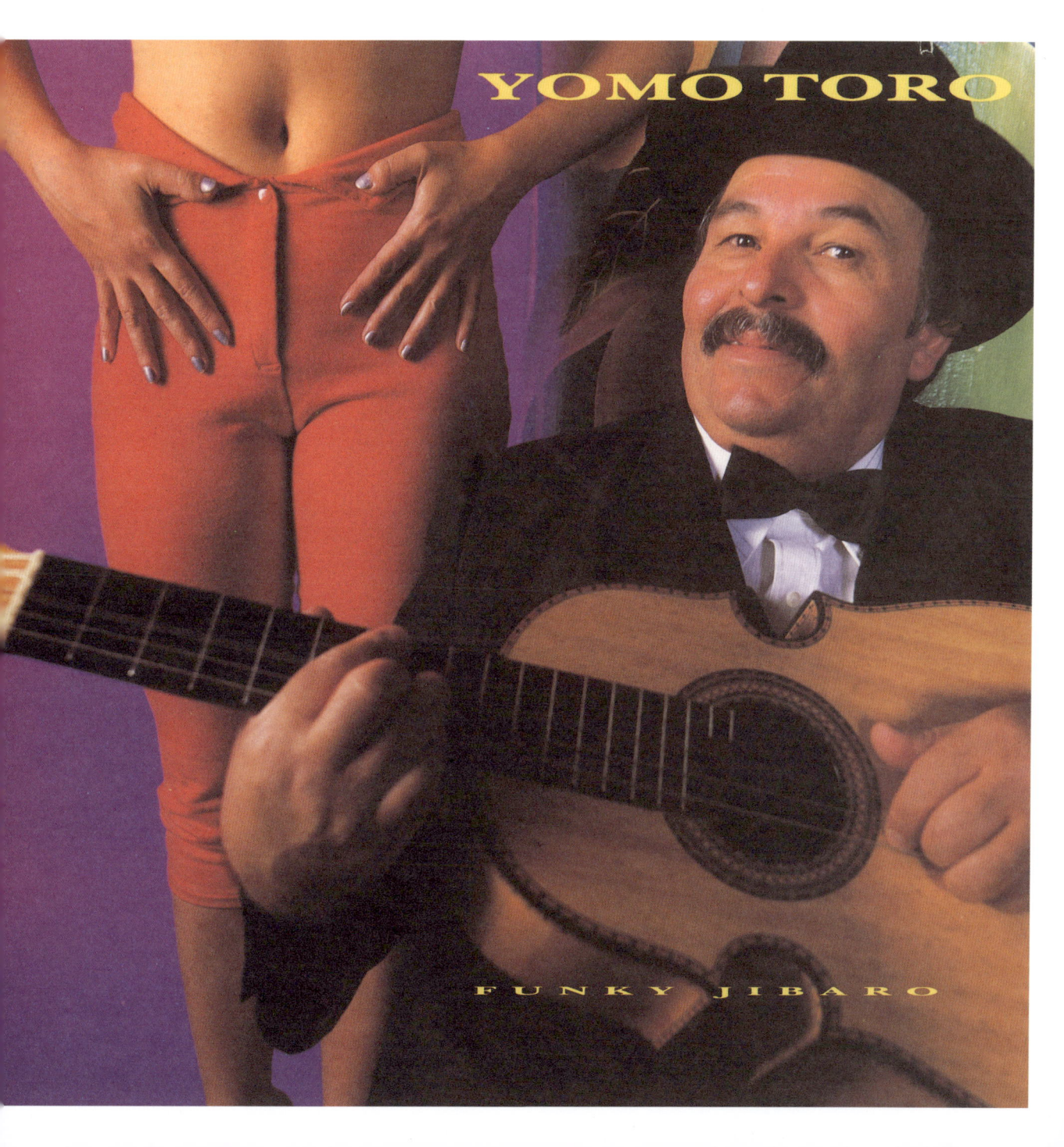

FUNKY JIBARO

JM-558
SERIES 0798

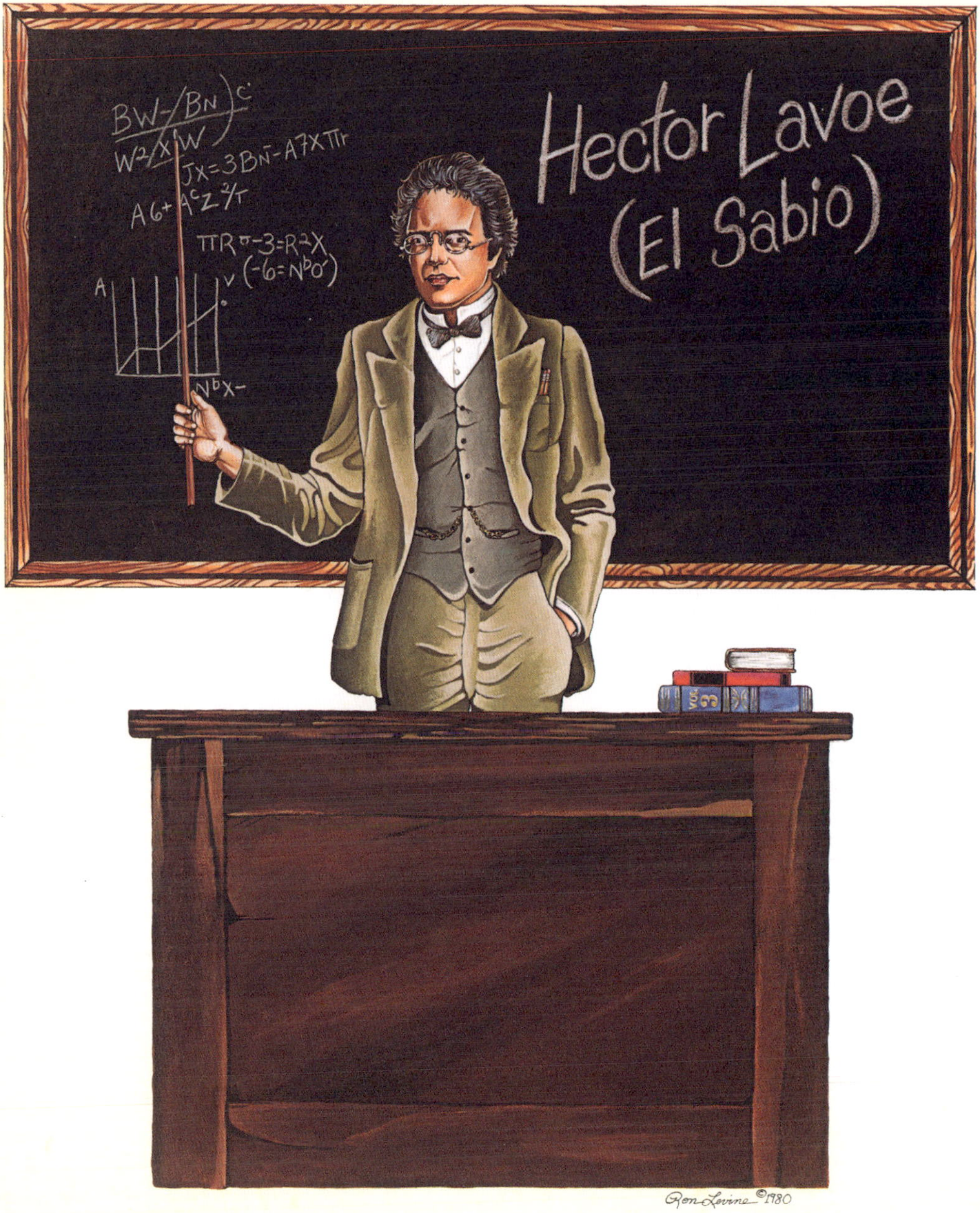

EL NEGRO NO TIENE NA

LOS VAN VAN

DAN
DEN

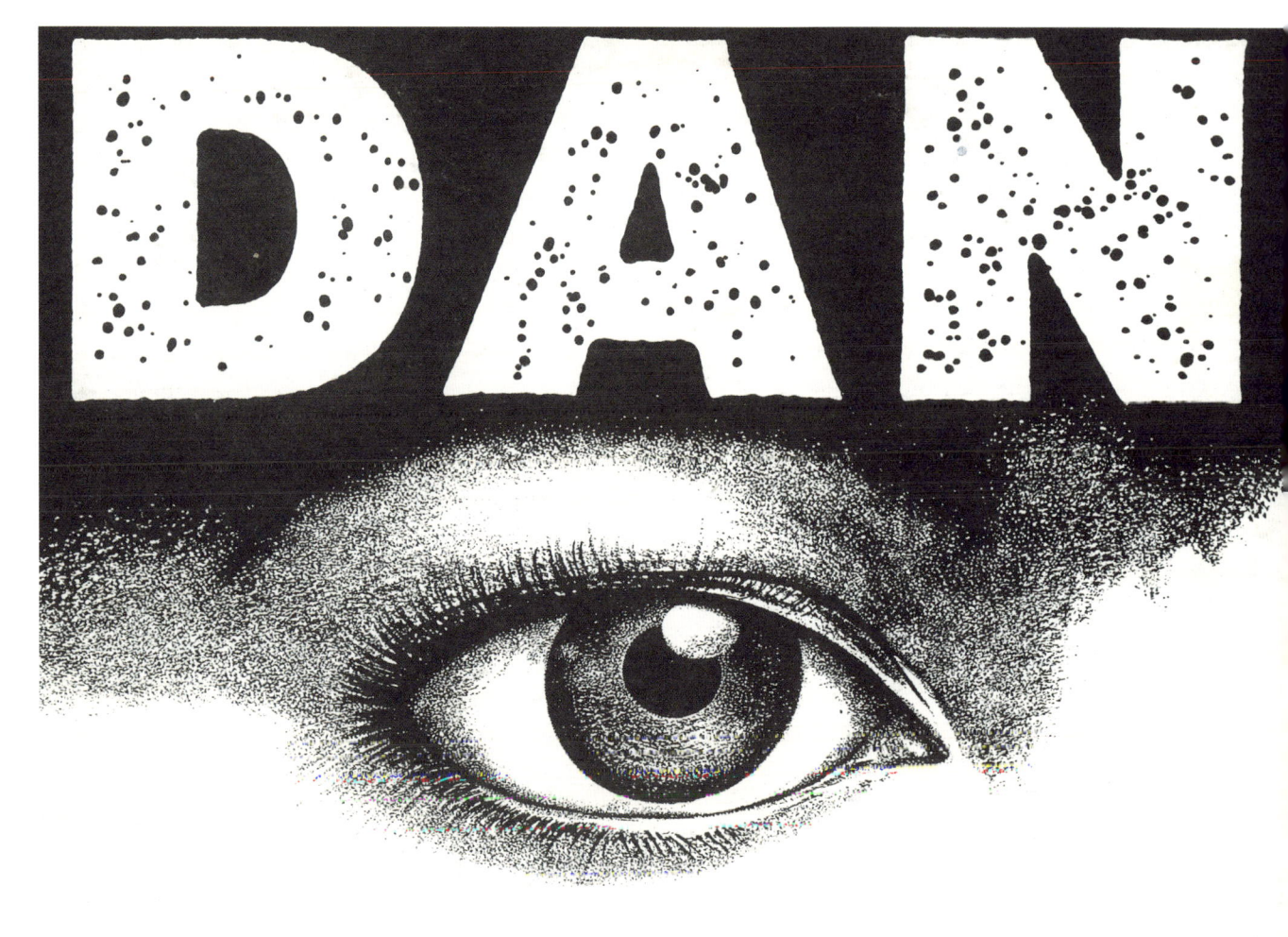

yerba buena

SONORA PONCEÑA

FUTURE

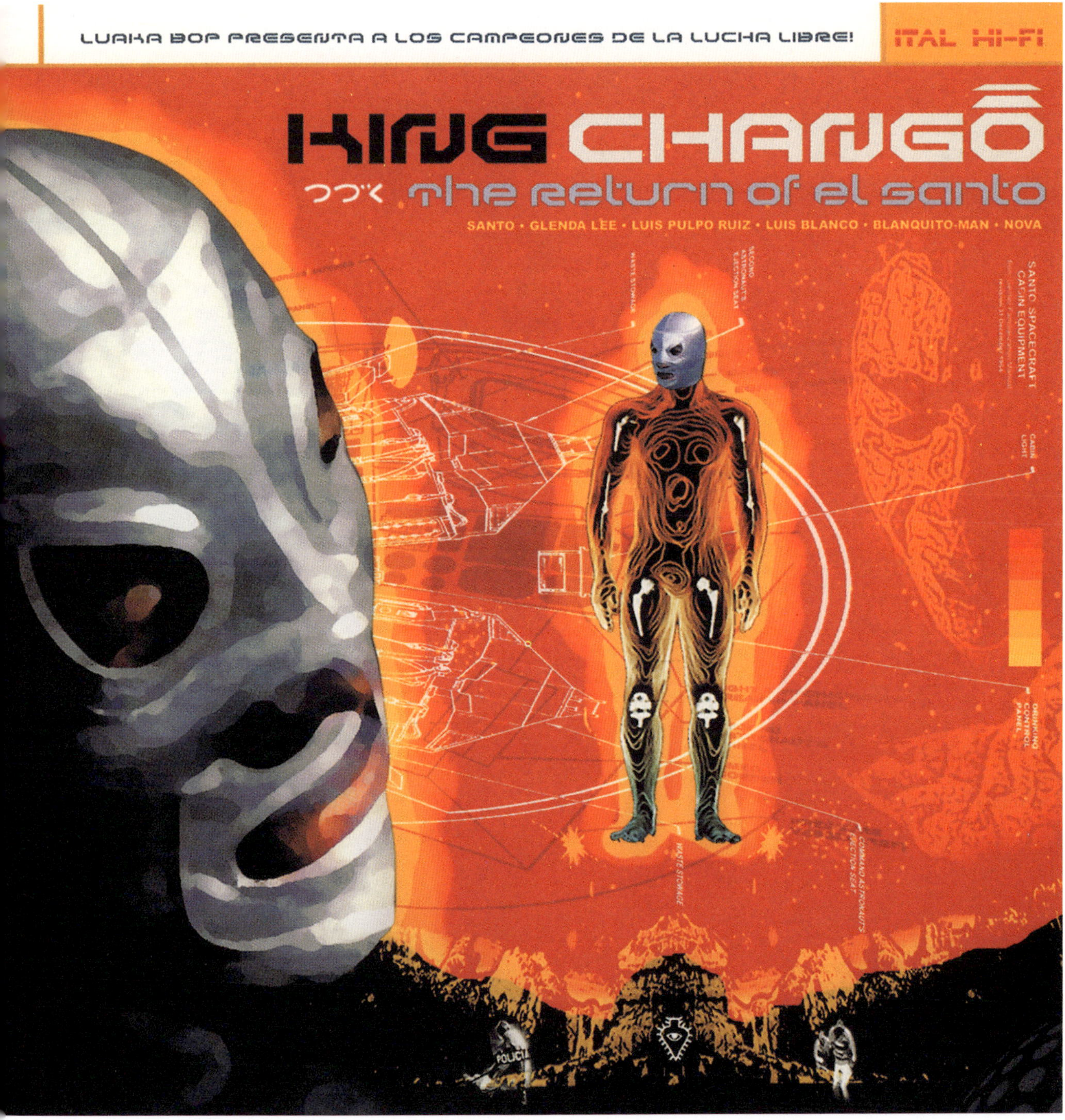
LUAKA BOP PRESENTA A LOS CAMPEONES DE LA LUCHA LIBRE!
ITAL HI-FI
KING CHANGÔ
the return of el santo
SANTO • GLENDA LEE • LUIS PULPO RUIZ • LUIS BLANCO • BLANQUITO-MAN • NOVA
SANTO SPACECRAFT CABIN EQUIPMENT
WASTE STOWAGE
SECOND ASTRONAUTS EJECTION SEAT
CABIN LIGHT
DRINKING CONTROL PANEL
WASTE STOWAGE
COMMAND ASTRONAUTS EJECTION SEAT
POLICIA

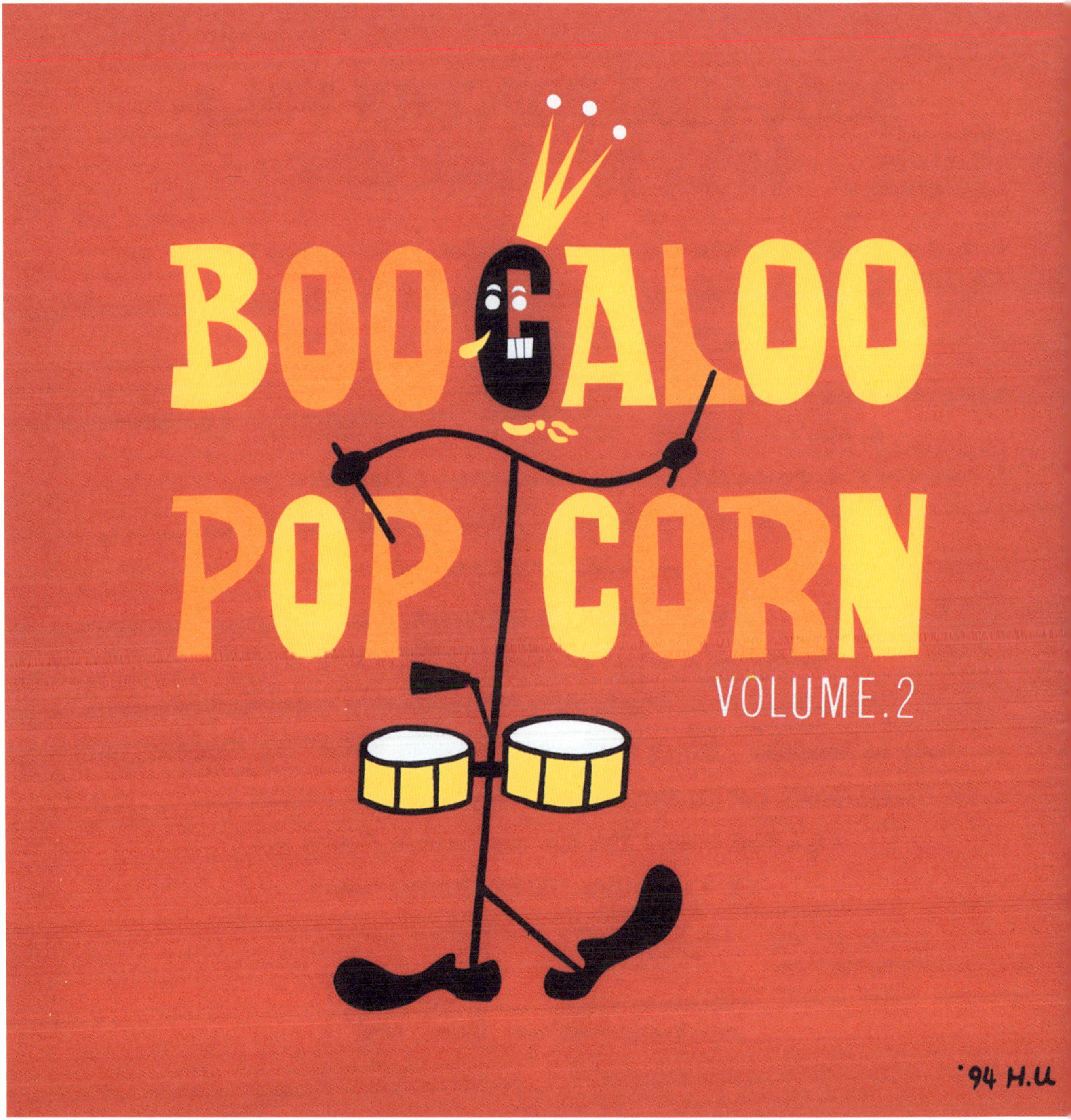
BOOGALOO
POPCORN
VOLUME.2
'94 H.U

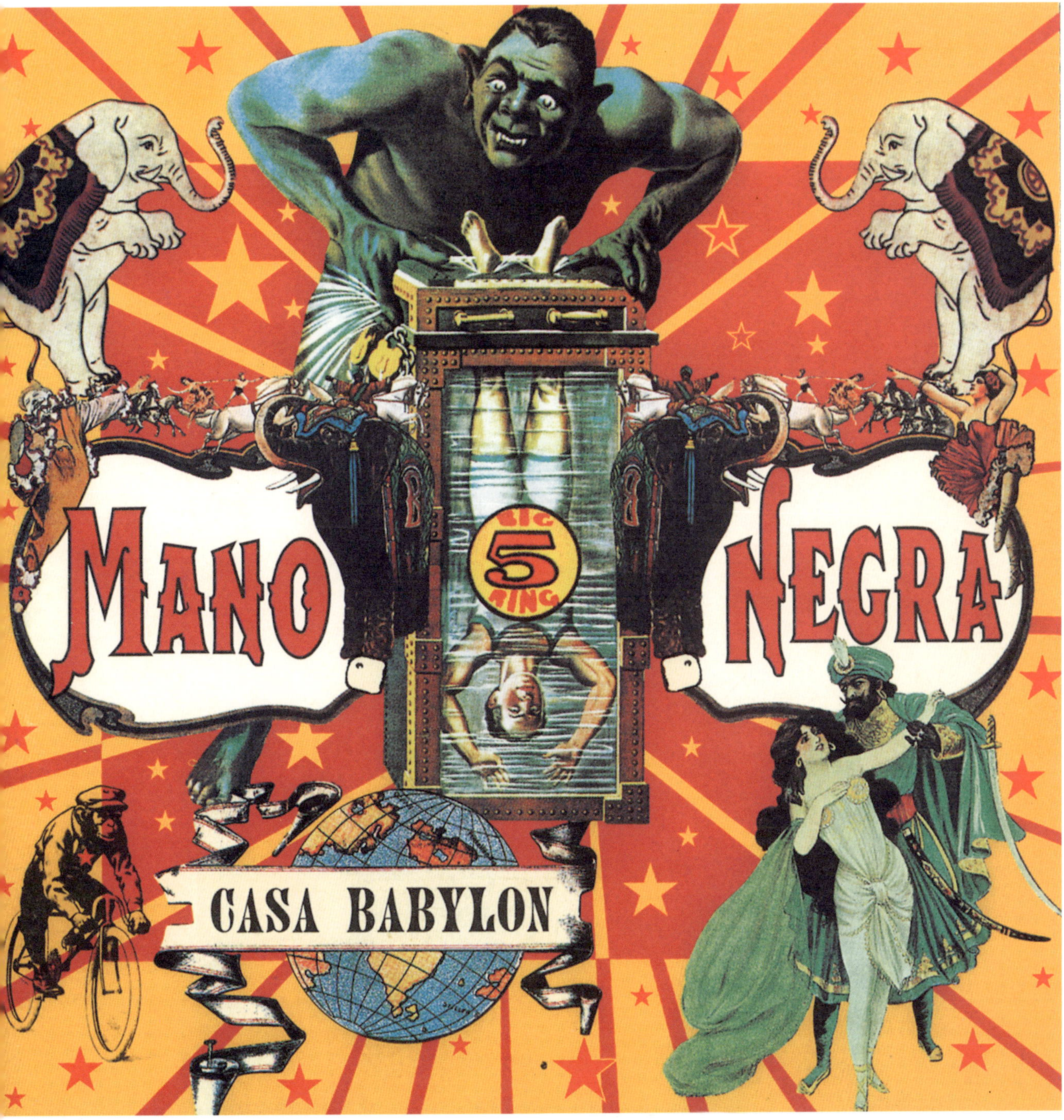
MANO
NEGRA
BIG 5 RING
CASA BABYLON

AFRICANDO

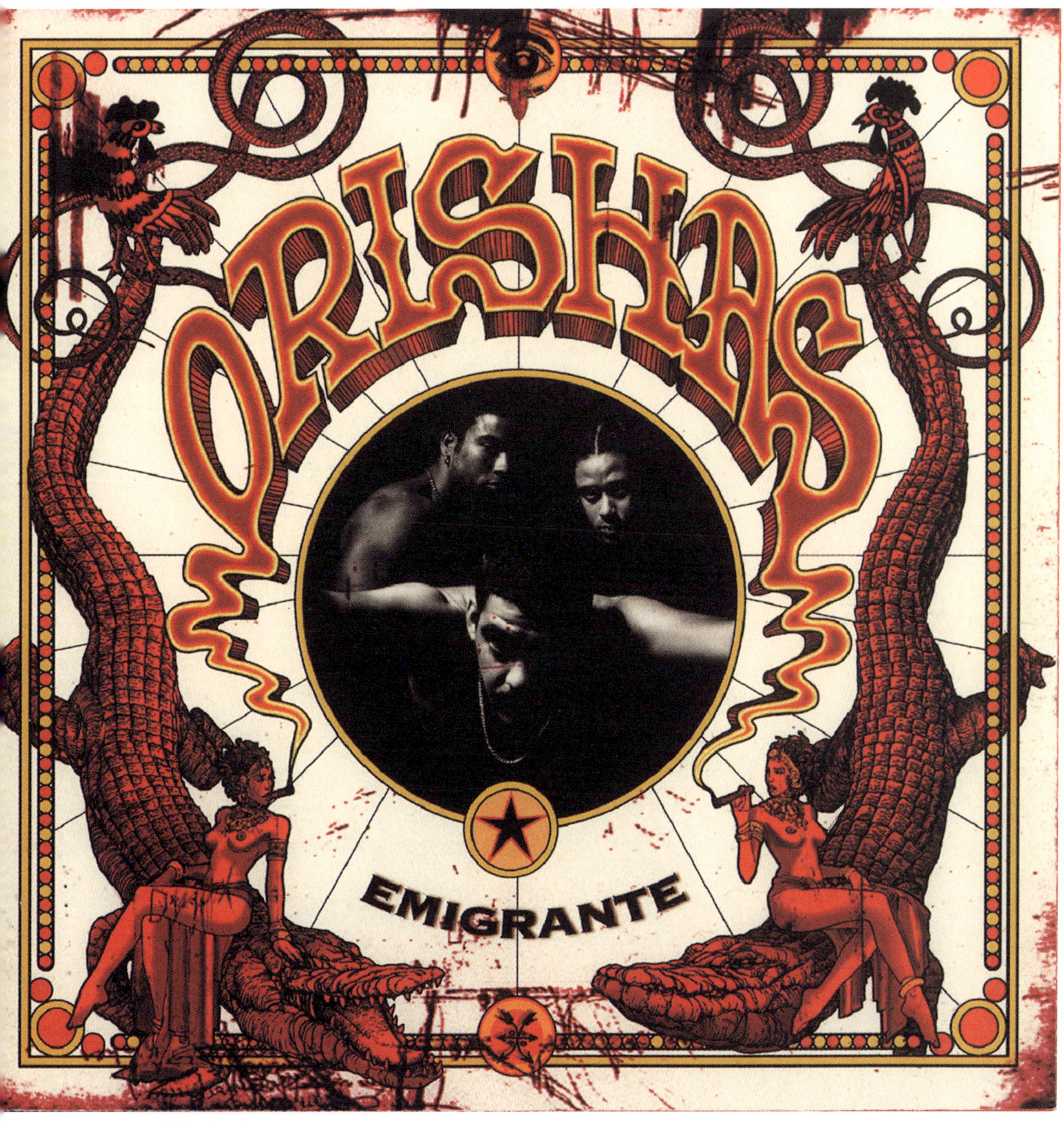
ORISHAS
EMIGRANTE

VOCAL SAMPLING

una forma mas

El Son No Ha Muerto
the best of Cuban Son

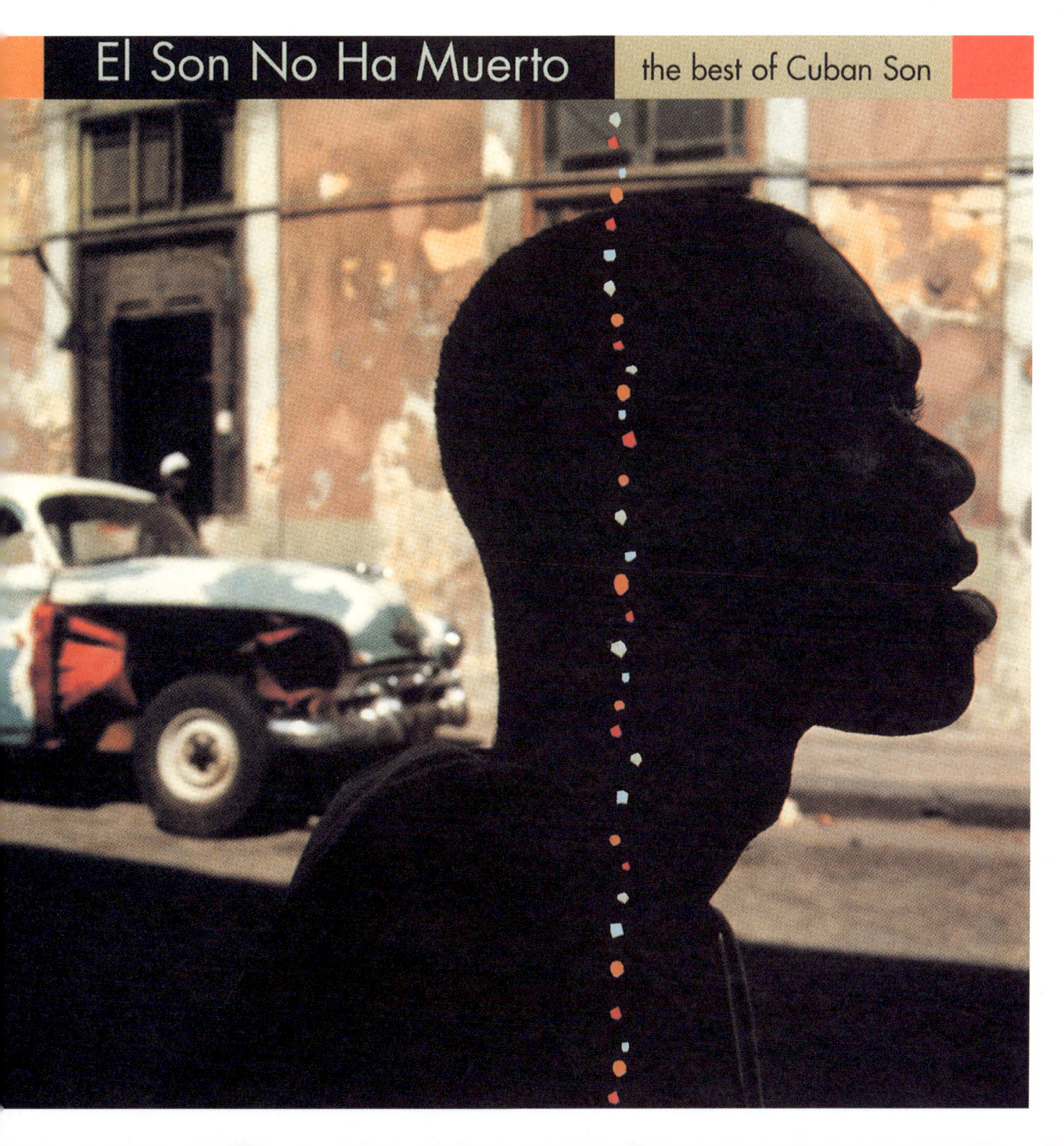

NICHE

ME HUELE A MATRIMONIO

FLORES

CONJUNTO CÉSPEDES

FEATURING: ROY AYERS, GEORGE BENSON, JOCELYN BROWN, INDIA, JAZZY JEFF, VINCENT MONTANA JR, EDDIE PALMIERI, TITO PUENTE

FABRICA DE NUEVA YORK DE

NUYORICAN SOUL

NUYORICAN SOUL

A production by Masters At Work

LOS LOBOS
Good Morning Aztlán

BUENA ★ VISTA ★ SOCIAL ★ CLUB ★

PRESENTS

Ibrahim Ferrer

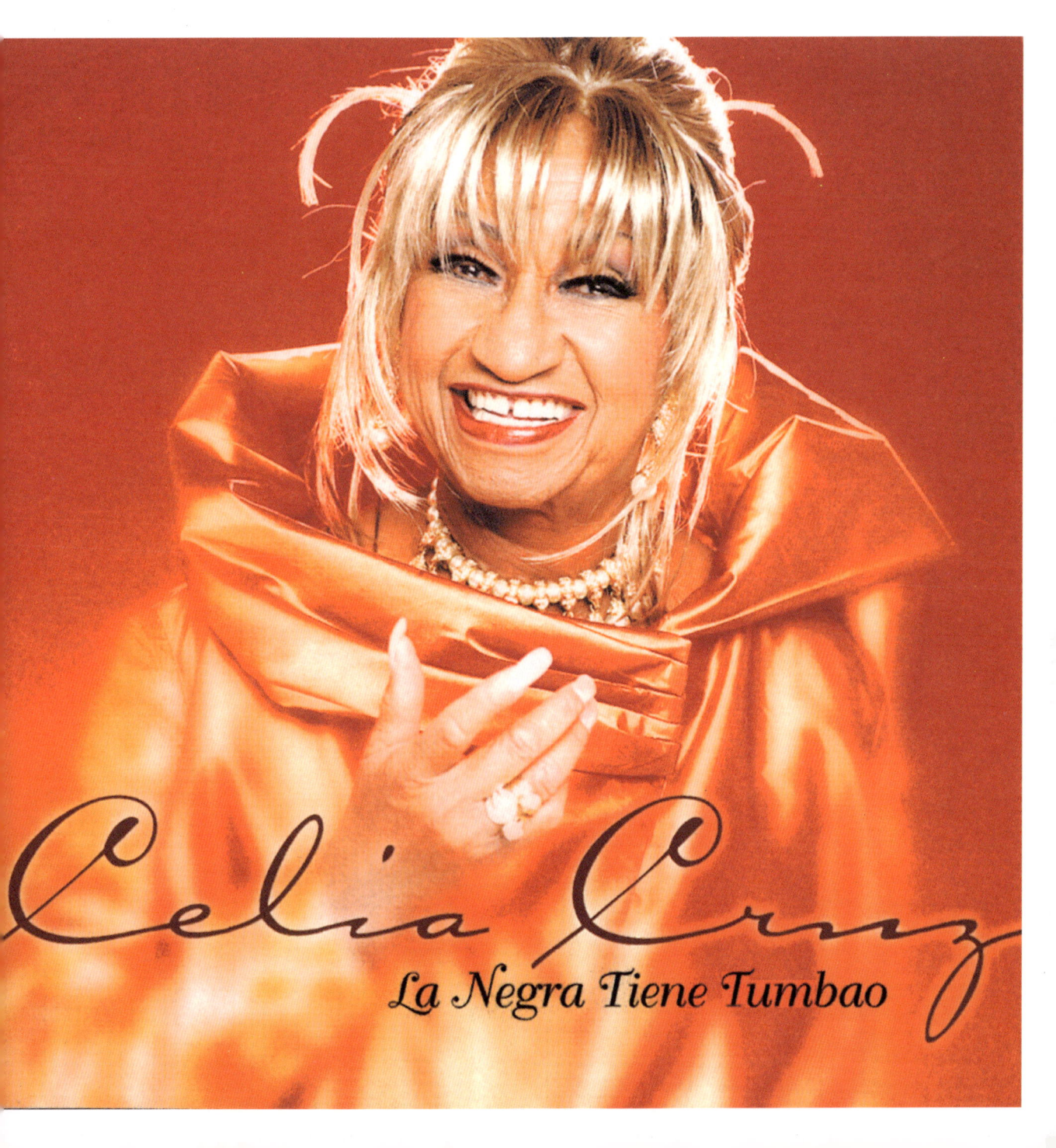

Celia Cruz
La Negra Tiene Tumbao

SWINGER RECORDS

ALEGRE RECORDS

Ansonia LONG PLAYING HIGH FIDELITY

VAYA RECORDS INC.

ATLANTIC

INCA

Leon

TICO RECORDS

RICO RECORDS

HIGH FIDELITY ORFEON ALTA FIDELIDAD

LAMPE RECORDS

FANIA RECORDS

TICO KING OF THE CHA CHA MAMBO

MIAMI RECORDS

Areito

TROPICAL ALTA FIDELIDAD

Ansonia LONG PLAYING HIGH FIDELITY

COLUMBIA

ALEGRE

ANTILLA

MOCAMBO

A&M RECORDS

COMPATIBLE STEREO ARTOL RECORDS

Verve

kapp

RMM

TI CO HIGH FIDELITY

EMBAJADOR DISCOS

L. HARLOW Productions

RCA

PALLADIUM
LATIN JAZZ & DANCE RECORDS

EGREM
EMPRESA DE GRABACIONES Y EDICIONES MUSICALES LA HABANA CUBA

Fantasy Records ®

CLEF RECORDS

PABLO ®

SUARITOS

RAY BARRETTO Productions

SEECO

Odeon
ODEON
ALTA FIDELIDADE

coco records

DISCOS NINFA

MARDI GRAS RECORDS

LA RAZA

FANIA

Musart

UA LATINO ™

HARVEY AVERNE MANAGEMENT LTD.

CAYTRONICS

BRONJO
DIVISION OF SEECO RECORDS, INC

SMC Pro-Arte

COTIQUE

TH top hits

messidor ™

maype

GNP Crescendo RECORDS

Capitol RECORDS

Salsoul ®

PHILIPS

HIGH FIDELITY
Panart RECORDS

WORLD CIRCUIT

RIVERSIDE

GEMA RECORDS

Discography

MAMBO MANIA

Carlos Molina
Rhumba with Carlos Molina and His Music of the Americas
Capitol, c. 1940
Art and design: Booth

Desi Arnaz and His Orchestra
Babalú and Seven Other Favorites
RCA Victor P 198, c. 1940

Orquesta Folklorica de Cuba
Festival del Danzón
Musart M114, c. 1950s

Beny Moré
Canciones de las Antillas
RCA Victor MLK 3085, c. 1950s

Pedro Infante
Pedro Infante canta La Calandria y otras canciones con el Mariachi Guadalajara
Peerless LPP 060

Orquesta Aragón
Cha Cha Cha
RCA Victor MLK 3070, c. 1950s

Joe Loco and his Quintet
Viva Mambo
Tico LP 1013, 1954
Art and design: Sandoval, Lee-Myles Assoc.

Various Artists
Discoteca Latina Presenta: Tito Rodriguez, Joe Loco, Alfredito, Tito Puente, Machito, Martino Savanto
El Globo 6006

Tito Puente and His Orchestra
Dance the Cha Cha Cha
Tico LP 1010
Photo: Jack Zwillinger

Yma Sumac
Voice of the Xtabay
Capitol H224, 1950
Photo: Tom Kelley

Arsenio Rodriguez y su conjunto
Sabroso y caliente
Antilla MLP 586

Trio Reynoso
A bailar Merengue con el Trio Reynoso
Tropical TRLP 4529, 1960
Art: T. Peralta

Charlie Palmieri, with La Playa Sextet and Emilio Reyes
Lo Ultimo
Embajador E6001

Pérez Prado and His Orchestra
Havana, 3 a.m.
RCA Victor LPM 1257, 1956

Mongo Santamaria
Watermelon Man!
Battle BM 6120, 1962
Photo: Mike Cuesta
Design: Ken Deardoff

Celia Cruz con La Sonora Matancera
Reflexiones de Celia Cruz con La Sonora Matancera
Seeco SCLP 92000, 1960
Photo: Audiomusica Mexico

Tito Puente
Pachanga con Puente
Tico LP 1083, 1961

Joe Cuba
Joe Cuba
Embajador E6003, c. 1960

Pacheco y su Charanga
Pacheco y su Charanga con Elliot Romero
Alegre LPA 801, c. 1961
Art and design: Izzy Sanabria

Fajardo, Chapotin, Orefiche, Conjunto Casino
Cuban Dance Festival: 4 Bands
Toreador T-539, c. 1966
Art and design: Ely Besalel

The Alegre All-Stars
The Alegre All-Stars Vol. 3: "Lost and Found"
Alegre SLPA 8430, 1966
Art and design: Izzy Sanabria

Juan Carlos Copes and Maria Nieves with Enrique Mendez and his Argentinian Orquesta
La Milonga
Patty LPP 102, 1960

Machito and His Orchestra
Si-si, no-no
Tico LP 1033, 1956
Design: Robert Brownjohn, Brownjohn, Chermayeff & Geismar

Los Admiradores
Bongos
Command/Grand Award
RS 809 SD, 1959
Art direction and design: Charles E. Murphy

Pérez Prado and His Orchestra
Dilo (Ugh!)
RCA Victor LPM 1883, 1958

Cuní con Chappotín y sus Estrellas
Musicalidad en sepia
Maype US 110, c. 1959
Design: Lee-Myles Assoc., Sendlein

CUBOP

Machito
Afro-Cuban Jazz: The Music of Chico O'Farrill
Clef MG C689, 1950
Design: David Stone Martin

Dizzy Gillespie and His Big Band featuring Chano Pozo
Gene Norman Presents: Dizzie Gillespie and His Big Band in Concert
GNP Crescendo GNPD 23, 1948/1993
Design: John Brandt

Cal Tjader Quintet
Cal Tjader Quintet
Fantasy 3232, 1956
Art and design: Betty Brader

Sabu Martinez
Sabu's Jazz Espagnole
Alegre, 1961
Art and design: Izzy Sanabria

Pete Terrace and His Latin Jazz Quintet
Mambo Jazz: The Nearness of You
Tico LP 1028, c. 1955
Design: Lee-Myles Assoc.
Photo: Jack Zwillinger

The George Shearing Quintet
Latin Escapade
Capitol T 737, 1956

Cal Tjader Quintet
Mambo with Tjader!
Fantasy 3326, c. 1956
Art and design: Wanek

Cándido Camero
Cándido in Indigo
ABC-Paramount ABC 236, c. 1960s
Design: F. Scott/F. Schutz
Photo: Myron Miller

Cachao y su Ritmo Caliente
Cuban Jam Sessions in Miniature: "Descargas"
Panart 2092, 1957

Tito Puente
Puente in Percussion
Tico LP 1011, c. 1960s
Photo: Alfred Gescheidt

Mongo Santamaria
Mongo '70
Atlantic SD 1567, 1970
Photo: Joel Brodsky
Art and design: Stanislaw Zagorski

Luis Gasca
Collage
Fantasy F 9504, 1976
Art direction: Phil Carroll
Art: Jamie Putnam

Forbidden Cuba in the 80's: Grupo Afrocuba
Smooth Jazz Moods
RMM RMD82235, 1998
Art direction: Carlo Angelo Moralishvili
Design: Pablo Yglesias
Photo: Jorge Garcia Torres

Various Artists
World Pacific Presents the Music of Cuba: El jazz cubano
World Pacific/Capitol/Blue Note CDP 0777 7 80599 2 9, 1993
Art: Pablo Yglesias
Design: Patrick Roques

Poncho Sanchez
Afro-Cuban Fantasy
Concord Picante CCD 4847, 1998
Art: Viredo
Design: Darren Wong Design

Paquito D'Rivera
Paquito D'Rivera Presents: 40 Years of Cuban Jam Sessions
Messidor 15826, 1993
Design: Bernd Deutscher and K.Y. Jelly
Photo: Ricardo Betancourt

ORIZA

Silvestre, El Rey del Canto Afro Cubano y Su Orquesta
Oriza: Afro-Cuban Rhythms
Seeco CELP 4260, 1958
Art and design: L. Pearl

Mongo Santamaria
Drums and Chants
Vaya JMVS 0698, 1978
Art and design: Charlie Rosario
Typography: Folio Graphics

Ramito
El cantor de la montaña
Ansonia ALP 1237

Various Artists
Festival In Havana
Riverside RLP 4005, 1955
Design: Gene Gogerty

Mongo Santamaria
Mongo Santamaria's Afro-Cuban Drums
SMC LP 592, 1952

Celina-Reutilio y Gina Martin
Fiesta Santera
Suaritos S 110, c. 1960s

Various Artists
Fiesta Santera: Toques y Cantos Santero Lucumi
Santero 375, c. 1960s

El Vive Bien con el Grupo Folklorico de Alberto Zayas
Guaguanco Afro-Cubano
Panart LP 2055

Jaime de Jesus y su cuarteto "Alma Alegre"
El Plenero
Ninfa NLP 03. 1952
Art and photo: R. Oliva
Design: Hispanoamerica Advertising Agency

Los Pleneros de la 21/Conjunto Melodia Tropical
Puerto Rico Puerto Rico Mi Tierra Natal
Shanachie 65001, 1990
Art: Manny Vega

La Lupe
La Lupe es la reina/La Lupe: The Queen
Tico LP 1192, 1969
Design: Ely Besalel
Photo: Warren Flagler

Emilio Barreto
Santisimo en ritual
Luz Productions LUZ 0002, 2001
Design: Pablo Yglesias

Trio Los Condes
Trio Los Condes
Gema/Aponte, c. 1960s

Sabu Martinez
Palo Congo
Blue Note BLT 1561, 1951
Design: Reid Miles
Photo: Francis Wolff

Luis Carbonell
Estampas de Luis Carbonell
Kubaney MT 119, c. 1950s

Cortijo y Kako
Ritmos y Cantos Callejeros
Ansonia SALP 1477, 1970

Carlos "Patato" Valdez and Eugenio "Totico" Arango
Patato & Totico
Verve V/V6-5037 LAT 10,006, c. 1960s
Design: Acy R. Lehman
Photo: Irv Elkin

Mongo Santamria
Up from the Roots
Atlantic SD 1621, 1972
Concept: Izzy Sanabria
Art direction and design: Richard Mantell

Daniel Ponce
New York Now!
Celluloid/OAO CELL 5005, 1983
Design: Felipe Orrego
Typesetting: Elliott Dunderdale
Layout: Thi-Linh Le

VIVA SOUL
Orchestra Harlow
Heavy Smokin'
Fania 331, 1966
Art direction: Izzy Sanabria
Photo: Lee Kraft

Joe Cuba
Wanted Dead or Alive/Se busca muerto o vivo
Tico LP 1146, 1966

Joe Cuba Sextet
My Man Speedy!
Tico LP 1161, 1967

Johnny Zamot
Tell It Like It Is
Decca DL 74945

TNT Boys
Sex Symbols/Simbolos Sexuales
Cotique CS 1038
Art direction: Izzy Sanabria
Photo: Bradley Olman

Tito Puente and His Orchestra
El Rey Tito Puente/The King Tito Puente
Tico LP 1172, 1968
Concept and art: Charlie Rosario

Eddie Bastian and His Orchestra
Hippies Boogaloo
Hopes 885

Joe Bataan
Subway Joe
Fania SLP 345, 1968
Art direction: Izzy Sanabria
Photo: Marty Topp

Eduardo Davidson
Le-Frisson
Pop Art LP 150, 1965
Art direction: George Salfi

Orchestra Harlow
El Exigente
Fania LP 342, 1968
Art direction: Izzy Sanabria
Photo: Marty Topp

The LeBron Brothers
I Believe
Cotique CS 1022
Design: John Murello
Photo: Charles Stewart

Ray Barretto
Acid
Fania LP 346, 1967
Design: Izzy Sanabria
Photo: Marty Topp

The Latin Souls
Tiger Boo-Ga-Loo
Kapp KS 3553

Eddie Palmieri
Superimposition
Tico LP 1194, 1970
Art and design: Ely Besalel

Monguito "el Único" y su conjunto
De todo un poco
Fania LP 386
Art and design: Izzy Sanabria

The Harvey Averne Band
Brotherhood
Fania LP 379, 1970
Art and design: Izzy Sanabria

Willie Colón, canta Héctor LaVoe
Guisando (Doing a Job)
Fania LP 370, 1969
Design: Walter Velez
Art director: Izzy Sanabria
Photo: Marty Topp

Willie Bobo
Spanish Grease
Verve V/V6-8631, 1965
Design: Acy R. Lehman
Photo: Rudy Legname

Cal Tjader
Soul Sauce
Verve V/V6-8614, 1964
Design: Acy R. Lehman
Photo: Murray Laden

Eddie Palmieri
Justicia
Tico LP 1188, 1969
Design: Ely Besalel
Photo: Warren Flagler

Orchestra Harlow
Me and My Monkey
Fania LP 374, 1969
Concept: Larry Harlow
Design: Izzy Sanabria
Photo: Len Baumin

Jimmy Sabater
El hijo de Teresa/Teresa's Son
Tico LP 1211, 1970
Art and design: Izzy Sanabria

Mongo Santamaria
Feelin' Alright
Atlantic SD 8252, 1970
Art: Izzy Sanabria
Design: Haig Adishian

Ray Rodrigues and His Orchestra
Delusion
Alegre LPA-869, 1969
Art, design, and photo: Ely Besalel

Willie Bobo
Juicy
Verve V/V6-8685, 1967
Design: Acy R. Lehman
Photo: Rudy Legname

Willie Bobo
Uno dos tres/1 2 3
Verve V/V6-8648, 1966
Design: Acy R. Lehman
Photo: Charles Stewart

Tito Puente
Tito Puente en el Puente (Tito Puente on the Bridge)
Tico LP 1191, 1970
Design: Ely Besalel
Photo: Warren Flagler

ÉCHALE SALSITA
Willie Colón
The Good, The Bad, The Ugly
Fania XSLP 00484, 1975
Art and design: Ron Levine
Photo: Lee Marshall

Willie Colón
La Gran Fuga/The Big Break
Fania LP 394, 1971
Concept and design: Izzy Sanabria

Willie Colón
El Juicio
Fania (S)LP 00424, 1972
Art: Aggie Whelane
Design: Izzy Sanabria

Willie Colón and Rubén Blades
Willie Colón Presents Rubén Blades: Metiendo Mano!
Fania LP 500, 1977
Design: Izzy Sanabria
Photo: Mark Kozlowski
Title design: Pam Lessero

Willie Colón and Rubén Blades
Siembra
Fania JM00-537, 1978
Photo: J. P. Posse
Art: Irene Perlicz

Ray Barretto
Power
Fania LP 391, 1972
Art and design: Izzy Sanabria

Ray Barretto
Indestructible
Fania LP 00456, 1973
Design and shirt: Walter Velez/WE-2 Graphic Designs
Photo: Roberto Schneider

Ray Barretto
Que via la música
Fania, 1972
Art Direction: Izzy Sanabria
Concept and design: WE-2 Graphic Designs
Art: Walter Velez

Hector Rivera and His Orchestra
Lo máximo
Tico CLP 1324, 1974
Art and design: Izzy Sanabria, Yogi Rosario, WE-2 Graphic Design, Walter Velez

Azuquita y su Orquesta Melao
Pura salsa
Vaya VS-34, 1975
Art direction and design: Izzy Sanabria

Ralphy Santi y su conjunto
Ralphy Santi y su conjunto
TR 132X, 1977
Design: "The Big Red" Design Studio

Orchestra Harlow
Hommy: A Latin Opera
Fania LP 00425, 1973
Concept: Larry Harlow
Design: Izzy Sanabria, Walter Velez, WE-2 Graphic Designs
Photo: Larry Harlow, Jan Blom

Joe Cuba Sextet
Bustin' Out
Tico LP 1300, 1972
Design and photo: Ely Besalel

Joe Cuba
Cocinando la Salsa (Cookin' the Sauce)
Tico JMTS 1405, 1976
Design: Ron Levine
Photo: Lee Marshall

Mongo Santamaria
Sofrito
Vaya JMVS-53, 1976
Design: Ron Levine
Photo: Lee Marshall

Héctor Lavoe
Comedia
Fania JM 0052, 1978
Art direction: Alberta Dering
Photo: Yoshi Ohara
Design and layout: Michael Ginsburg/Gazebo Group

Ray Baretto
Rican/struction
Fania SLP 552, 1979
Concept, art direction, and design: Izzy Sanabria, Latin Communications, Inc.

Eddie Palmieri
The Sun of Latin Music
Coco LP 109XX, 1974
Art and design: Charlie Rosario
Photo: Gary Mason

Francisco "Kako" Bastor
Kako
TR LP 00900X, c. 1970s
Art, design, and photo: Charlie Rosario

Charlie Palmieri
ElectroDuro
Coco LP 111, 1974
Art and design: Charlie Rosario
Photo: Gary Mason

Larry Harlow
Live in Quad
Fania QXSLP 00472, 1974
Art and design: Charlie Rosario
Photo: Gary Mason

Conjunto Melao
Conjunto Melao
TR 113X, 1976
Concept, art, design, and photo: Charlie Rosario

Tipica '73
La candela
Inca XSLP 1043, 1975
Concept, art, and design: Charlie Rosario

Cortijo
Cortijo and His Time Machine/Cortijo y su Máquina de Tiempo
Coco LP 108, 1974
Concept, art, design, and photo: Ely Besalel

Ismael Rivera con sus cachimbos
Esto fue lo que trajo el barco
Tico LP 1305, 1972
Art and design: Ely Besalel

Tito Rodriguez and His Orchestra
Uptempo
Tico JMTS 1427, 1978
Art and design: Yogi Rosario

Grupo Folklorico y Experimental Nuevayorquino
Lo dice todo
Salsoul Sal 4110, 1976
Art direction, art, and photo: Yogi Rosario

Eddie Palmieri
Lucumi, Macumba, Voodoo
Epic 35523, 1978
Design: Paula Scher
Photo: Jim Houghton

Fania All-Stars
Live in Japan, 1976
Fania 116, 1976
Concept, art, and title lettering: Ron Levine

Oscar D'Leon
El Discóbolo
Top Hits TH-AMF 2207, 1982

Todos Estrellas
Siglo 1 A.N.E.
EGREM/Arieto LD 4340, 1986
Design and photo: Marucha

Sonora Ponceña
Sonora Ponceña
Inca LP 1033, 1972
Art direction: Izzy Sanabria
Art: Walter Velez
Design: WE-2 Graphic Designs

Sonora Ponceña
Energized
Inca JMIS-1072, 1979
Concept, art, and design: Ron Levine

OYE COMO VA

Santana
Abraxas
Columbia PC 30130, 1970
Art: Mati Klarwein
Photo: Marian Schmidt
Graphics: Bob Venosa

Santana
Santana
Columbia PC 9781, 1970
Art: Lee Konklin

Harlem River Drive
Harlem River Drive Featuring Eddie Palmieri and Jimmy Norman
Roulette SR 3004, 1971
Design: Ruby Mazur's Art Dept.
Photo: Leonard Freed

The Harvey Averne Barrio Band
The Harvey Averne Barrio Band
Heavy Duty LP 101, 1971
Concept: Harvey Averne
Front cover art: Ludovico de Luigi/Galleria d'Arte Moderna Ravagnan, Venice, Italy
Design: Izzy Sanabria
Back cover photo: Bob Gruen

The Jimmy Castor Bunch
It's Just Begun
RCA LSP 4640, 1972
Art direction: Acy R. Lehman
Art: Corrigan
Design: Frank Mulvey

Mandrill
Solid
United Artists/Gema UAS 29 786 XO, 1975

Concept: Bob Cato and Mandrill
Art: Papio Sphinx
Design: Bob Cato

Seguida
Love Is...
Fania XSLP 00478, 1974
Concept: Bill Garretson
Art and design: Izzy Sanabria

Mongo Santamaria
Afro-Indio
Vaya XVS 38, 1975
Art and design: Ron Levine

El Chicano
Revolución
Kapp KS 3640, 1971
Art direction: John C. LeProvost
Design: Virginia Clark
Photo: Eddie Caballero

El Chicano
Celebration
Kapp/MCA KS 3663, 1972
Photo: Richard Rankin

Azteca
Pyramid of the Moon
Columbia KC 32451, 1973
Design and photo: Bruce Steinberg

Malo
Malo
Warner Bros. BS 2584, 1972
Art direction: Chris Whorf
Art: Jesus Helguera/Galas de Mexico, S.A.
Design: John and Barbara Casado

Bwana
Bwana
Caytronics CYS 1312, 1972
Art direction: Manuel Vega F.
Design: Bwana

Cándido
Thousand Finger Man
Solid Sate SS 18066, 1969
Art direction: Frank Gauna
Photo: Chuck Stewart

Toro
Toro
Coco LP 106, 1975
Art direction: Izzy Sanabria
Design: Chico Alvarez
Art: Walter Velez

Santana
Santana's Greatest Hits
Columbia PC 33050, 1974
Design: John Berg
Photo: Joel Baldwin

OH, MEU BRASIL
Various Artists
Carnival '62
RCA BBL-1162, 1962

Clara Petraglia
Brazil
Westminster WF 12024
Photo: Maria Martel

Various Artists
3rd festival da música popular brasileira, vol. 1
Philips R765.014L, 1967

João Gilberto
The Boss of the Bossa Nova
Atlantic 8070, 1965
Photo: Jim Marshall
Design: Loring Eutemey

Moreira da Silva
Conversa de Botequim
Imperial/EMI-Odeon IPM 30196, 1966
Art: Miéco Caffé

Various Artists
Tropicália ou panis et circenis
Philips R765.040L, 1968
Photo: Rubens Gerchman

Tom Zé
Tom Zé
Rozenblit LP 50.010, 1968
Art: Satoru
Design and photo: Officina Programação Visual-SP

Gilberto Gil
Gilberto Gil
Philips R765.087L, 1969
Art and design: Rogério Duarte, Antônio Dias
Photo: David Drew Zingg

Caetano Veloso
Caetano Veloso
Philips R765.026L, 1968
Art: Liana and Paulo Tavares
Layout: Rogério Duarte
Photo: David Drew Zingg

Maria Bethânia
Recital na boite barroco
Odeon MOFB 3545, 1968
Art: Luiz Jasmin
Design: Joel

Jorge Ben
Jorge Ben
Philips R765.100L, 1969
Art: Albery
Design: Lincoln
Photo: Johnny Salles

Gal Costa
Legal
Philips R765.126L, 1970
Art, design, and photos: Hélio Oiticica

Secos & molhados
Secos & molhados
Continental LP 10112, 1973

Baden Powell
Images on Guitar
MPS 29057, 1973
Design: Wolfgang Baumann
Photo: MPS-Frey, VARIG: B. Valentien, K. H. Niemeyer

João Bosco
Caça à raposa
RCA Victor 103.0112
Design and art:
Galuco Rodrigues
Art direction: Ney Tavora
Photo: Ivan Klingen
Art and layout: Glauco Rodrigues

Luiz da Muriçoca
Cânticos de terreiro
Philips/Compania Brasileira de Discos 632.943, 1971
Art and layout: Nilo Jorge/Matiz

Ilê Aiyê
Canto negro
Polygram/Odebrecht, 1984
Art: J. Cunha
Design: Frederico Mendes

Various Artists
Documentos foclóricos Brasileiros: Candomble 1
Editora Xauã XM1
Design: Carybé (Hector Bernabó)
Layout: José Medeiros
Photo: Salomão Scliar

Paul Horn
Altura do Sol (High Sun)
Epic PE 34231, 1976
Art: Carol Wald
Design: Ed Lee
Photo: Baron Wolman

Gal Costa
Índia (Sangue tupy pique)
Philips 6349077, 1973
Design: Edinizio Ribeiro
Photo: Antonio Guerreiro

Jorge Mautner
Antimaldito
Polygram 8249501, 1985
Design: Rogério Cavalcanti
Photo: Reinaldo Coser, Ayrton Camargo

Arrigo Barnabé E A Banda Sabor de Veneno
Clara crocodilo
Robinson Borba, 1980
Art and design: Luiz Gê
Photo: A. C. Tonelli

Tom Zé
Todos os olhos
Continental LP 10121
Concept: Décio Pignatari
Design: M. Pedro Ferreira
and F. Eduardo de Andrade
Photo: Reinaldo de Moraes

BARRIO NUEVO
Various Artists
Barrio Nuevo
Soul Jazz SJR LP 45, 1999
Design: Adrian Self and Steve Snowglobe
Photo: Don Hunstein

Kid Frost
East Side Story
Virgin 2-92097, 1992
Art direction: Steve Gerdes
Art: Cartoon
Design: Steve Gerdes and Tom Dolan

Rubén Blades y Seis del Solar
Escenas (Scenes)
Elektra 9 60432, 1985
Concept: Rubén Blades and Ricardo Betancourt
Art direction: Roberto Mercado
Design and photo: Ricardo Betancourt

Rubén Blades y Seis del Solar
Buscando América
Elektra 60352, 1984
Design: Jorge Vargas
Photo: Ricardo Betancourt

Yomo Toro
Funky Jibaro
Antilles/New Directions 90693, 1988
Photo: Abe Frajndalich

Héctor Lavoe
El Sabio
Fania JM 558, 1980
Art and design: Ron Levine

Los Van Van
El negro no tiene na
Egrem LD 4497, 1988

Juan Carlos y El Dan Den
Siempre hay un ojo que te ve
Arieto/Egrem LD 4670, 1990
Design: Alberto Soria
Art: Jams

Yerba Buena
President Alien
Razor & Tie/Fun Machine 7930182894, 2003
Design: Chris Capuozzo and Jeff Jackson for Funny Garbage
Photo: Mark Seliger
Photo imaging: Alex Martinegro

Sonora Ponceña
Future
Inca JMI 1081, 1984
Concept, art, and design: Ron Levine

King Changó
The Return of El Santo
Luaka Bop 72438-50307-2-7, 2000
Art direction, design, photo: Andres Blanco for Big Mama and Collectivo Design Group

Various Artists
Boogaloo Popcorn Volume 2
P-Vine/Blues Interactions, Inc. R 440305, 1994
Art: Hirosuke "Amore" Ueno

Mano Negra
Casa Babylon
Virgin France, S.A. PM 527 396552, 1994
Art and design: Manu Chao

Africando
Vol. 1: Trovador
Stern's STCD 1045, 1993
Art: Svetlana Yavorskaya
Design: Affiche Rouge
Photo: Fred Marcus Inc.

Orishas
Emigrante
Surco 440 018 456, 2002
Design: Edouard Salier
Art: Antoine Audagiori
Photo: Michel Momy

Vocal Sampling
Una forma más
Sire 61792, 1995
Art direction and design: Linda Cobb
Photo: F. Scott Schafer

Various Artists
El Son No Ha Muerto: The Best of Cuban Son
Rhino R2 76719, 2001
Design: Julie Vlasak
Photo: Jimmy Dorantes/Latin Focus.com

Grupo Niche
Me huele a matrimonio
Codiscos 298 21061, 1986
Design: Jaime Uribe & Asoc.

Conjunto Cespedes
Flores
Xenophile/Green Linnet Xeno 4043, 1998
Art: Calef Brown
Design: Greenberg Kingsley

Nuyorican Soul
Nuyorican Soul
Giant Step/Blue Thumb GSRD 1130, 1997
Concept: Candace Strickland
Design: Green Ink

Los Lobos
Good Morning Aztlán
Mammoth 2061-65518, 2002
Art direction: Louie Pérez, Al Quattrocchi, and Jeff Smith
Design: Tornado Design
Art: Sandow Birk

Ibrahim Ferrer
Buena Vista Social Club Presents: Ibrahim Ferrer
Nonesuch 79532, 1999
Design: The Team
Photo: Karl Haimel

Celia Cruz
La negra tiene tumbao
Sony Discos TRK-84519/2-503154, 2001
Design: Mario Houben
Photo: Adolfo Pérez Butron

Bibliography

Carr, Leroy. *A Century of Jazz*. New York: Da Capo Press, 1997.

Chapman, Rob, et. al. *Album Covers from the Vinyl Junkyard*. London: Booth-Clibborn Editions, 1997.

Cuesta, Maggy. *¡Propaganda!* New York: American Institute of Graphic Arts, 2001.

Daver, Manek. *Jazz Album Covers: The Rare and the Beautiful*. Tokyo: Graphic Sha Publishing, 1994.

Duarte, Rogério, and Narlan Matos. *Tropicaos*. Rio de Janeiro: Azougue Press, 2003.

Dunn, Christopher. *Brutality Garden*. Chapel Hill: University of North Carolina Press, 2001.

Espada, Martín. *Alabanza: New and Selected Poems, 1982–2002*. New York: W. W. Norton & Company, 2003.

Fernández, Raúl. *Latin Jazz: The Perfect Combination/La Combinación Perfecta*. San Francisco: Chronicle Books, 2002.

Flores, Juan. *From Bomba to Hip-Hop: Puerto Rican Culture and Latino Identity*. New York: Columbia University Press, 2000.

Foehr, Stephen. *Dancing with Fidel*. London: Sanctuary Publishing, 2001.

Gleason, Judith, *Agotime, Her Legend*, with drawings by Carybé. New York: Grossman Publishers, 1970.

Klarwein, Mati. *Mil Ventanas/A Thousand Windows*. Deià de Mallorca, Spain: Max Publishing, 1995.

Leymarie, Isabelle. *Cuban Fire*. London and New York: Continuum, 2002.

Morales, Ed. *The Latin Beat: The Rhythms and Roots of Latin Music from Bossa Nova to Salsa and Beyond*. New York: Da Capo Press, 2003.

Pérez, Jr., Louis A. *On Becoming Cuban: Identity, Nationality, and Culture*. Chapell Hill: University of North Carolina Press, 1999.

Perron, Charles A. *Masters of Contemporary Brazilian Song*. Austin: University of Texas Press, 1989.

Perron, Charles A., and Christopher Dunn. *Brazilian Popular Music and Globalization*. Gainesville: University Press of Florida, 2001.

Polin, Bruce, et al. *Descarga 98/99 Catalog*. New York: www.Descarga.com, 1999.

Reyes, David, and Tom Waldman. *Land of a Thousand Dances: Chicano Rock 'n' Roll from Southern California*. Albuquerque: University of New Mexico Press, 1998.

Roberts, John Storm. *Latin Jazz: The First of the Fusions, 1880s to Today*. New York: Schirmer Books, 1999.

———. *The Latin Tinge: The Impact of Latin American Music on the United States*. New York: Oxford University Press, 1979.

Rothenstein, Julian, and Mel Gooding. *The Playful Eye: An Album of Visual Delight*. San Francisco: Chronicle Books, 1999.

Roy, Maya. *Cuban Music*. Princeton, NJ: Marcus Wiener Publishers, 2002.

Salazar, Max. *Mambo Kingdom: Latin Music in New York*. New York: Schirmer Trade Books, 2002.

Sanabria, Izzy. *Salsa Magazine*. http://www.salsamagazine.com.

Sanabria, Izzy, et al. "Twelve Years of *Latin N.Y.*/Art That…Spoke to the World!" *Latin N.Y.* (10), 1984.

Schreiner, Claus. *Música Brasileira*. New York: Marion Boyars Publishers, 2002.

Steward, Sue, *¡Música! Salsa, Rumba, Merengue, and More*, with foreword by Willie Colón. San Francisco: Chronicle Books, 1999.

Sweeny, Philip. *The Rough Guide to Cuban Music*. London, Rough Guides, 2001.

Thompson, Robert Farris. *Flash of the Spirit: African & Afro-American Art & Philosophy*. New York: Vintage Books, 1984.

———. *Face of the Gods: Art and Altars of Africa and the African Americas*. New York: Museum for African Art, Munich: Prestel, 1993

Thorgerson, Storm, and Aubrey Powell. *100 Best Album Covers*. New York: DK Publishing, 1999.

Toop, David. *Exotica*. London: Serpent's Tail, 1999

———. *Rap Attack, No. 3*. London: Serpent's Tail, 2000.

Veloso, Caetano. *Tropical Truth*. New York: Alfred A. Knopf, 2002.

Yglesias, Luis. *My Father's House*. Cambridge, MA: Identity Press, 1967.

Acknowledgments

The publishers: Kevin Lippert, editors Mark Lamster and Scott Tennent, designer Deb Wood, and the staff at PAP. You believed in me, an unpublished graphic designer and DJ, and my dedication to Latino music and culture. Your faith that this important part of music culture warranted publication in book form made it all possible.

The collectors: Harvey Averne, Emilio Barreto, Ely Besalel, Christopher Dunn, Teddy Fire, Randall Heath (for the scans), Joseph "DJ Joey Acevedo" Krupczynski, Ron Levine, Brandon Marger, Morton Marks, Charles A. Perrone, Knox Robinson, Hermán Rodriguez-Bajandas, Charlie Rosario, Brendon "DJ Ándujar" Rule, Izzy Sanabria, Fred Schmalz, Glenn Siegal, Robert Farris Thompson, Sarah Wulff, and Luis Yglesias. Thank you for broadening my horizons with your knowledge, collections, and generosity. Also thanks to the following stores (some now defunct): Academy (NYC), Amoeba (SF), Bate (NYC), Blue Angel (Miami), Casa Latina (NYC), Crocodilo (Madrid), Dusty Groove (Chicago), Dynamite (Northampton), Ear Wax (Brooklyn), Final Vinyl (NYC), Jazz Record Center (NYC), Groove Merchant (SF), In Your Ear (Boston; Providence), Mystery Train (Boston; Amherst), Planet (Boston), Pyramid (NYC), Record Mart (NYC), Round Again (Providence), The Sound Library (NYC), Sounds (NYC), Tower (NYC), Zambra (Barcelona), and of course César "Mr. Bugalú" at the Sixth Avenue Flea Market (NYC).

The interviewees: Harvey Averne, John Berg, Jorge Bermudez, Ely Besalel, Rubén Blades, Joe Cain, Joe Cuba, Rogério Duarte, Larry Harlow, Ron Levine, Morton Marks, Hansel Martinez, Narlan Matos, Ana de Oliveira, Charlie Palmieri II, Charlie Rosario, Yogi Rosario, Jimmy Sabater, Izzy Sanabria, Robert Farris Thompson, and Manny Vega. Without your patience and insight, the stories would never have been told.

The advisors and editors: Christopher Dunn and Morton Marks for their critical attention to detail. Alfredo Alvarado, Crisóbal Díaz Ayala, Emilio Barreto, Christoph Cox, Spencer Drate, Martín Espada, Tom Evored (Blue Note), Richard Foos (Rhino), DJ Fruitloop & DJ Diamond, Margot Glass, Mercedes Glass (Ansonia), Victor Gallo (Fania/Sonido), Randall Grass (Shanachie), Tabitha Griffin, Andy Kaufman, Craig Kallman (Atlantic), Denis Kitchen, Andrés Levin, René Lopez, Narlan Matos, Nick "Zip 8010," Michael Ochs, Ana de Oliveira, Rico Pavia, Charles Perrone, Hermán Rodriguez-Bajandas, Patrick Roques, Izzy Sanabria, Phil Scher, W. S. Tekweme, Robert Farris Thompson, Irv Tepper, Manny Vega, Yaster, and Luis Ellicott Yglesias. Thank you for your advice, guidance, and information.

The inspiration: my parents' love of Latin music and Latino cultures, my wife's indomitable spirit and sound judgment, the rock and jazz album cover books that initiated the genre, Spencer Drate's *45 RPM*, the quality covers and adventuresome spirit of Izzy Sanabria, Ely Besalel, Charlie Rosario, Ron Levine, and Rogério Duarte, plus the recordings and performances of people like Ray Barretto, Rubén Blades, Jorge Ben (Jor), Manu Chao, Willie Colón, Celia Cruz, Joe Cuba Sextet, Gilberto Gil, Los Lobos, Israel "Cachao" López, La Lupe, Mandrill, Orishas, Charlie and Eddie Palmieri, Tito Puente, Mongo Santamaria, Carlos Santana, Caetano Veloso, and Tom Zé—theirs is an art that paints pictures with words and music.

Credits

The author acknowledges the assistance and support of the following record labels who have generously allowed their album art to be reproduced in this volume:

ABC Paramount, Alegre, A&M, Ansonia, Antilla, Antilles/New Directions, Aponte, Arieto, Atlantic, Battle, Blue Note, Blue Thumb/Giant Step, Capitol, Capp, Caytronics, CBS, Celluloid, Charly, Coco, Codiscos, Columbia, Command, Concord Picante, Continental, Cotique, CTI, Decca, Demon Music Group, El Globo, Egrem, Elektra/Asylum, Embajador, EMI, Epic, Fania, Fantasy, Fun Machine, Gema, GNP Crescendo, GRP, Harmless, Hopes, Imperial, Inca, Kubaney, Luaka Bop, Mammoth, Maype, MCA, Mercury, Messidor, MGM, Miami, Mocambo, MPS, Musart, Nascente, Natasha, Ninfa, Nonesuch, Odebrecht, Odeon, Orfeón, Panart, Patty, Philips, Polygram, Pop Art, P-Vine, Razor & Tie, RCA Victor, RGE, Rhino, Riverside, Rosenblit, Roulette, RMM, Ryco Latino, Salsoul, Seeco, Shanachie, Sire, SMC, Solid State, Sonido, Sony Tropical, Soul Jazz, Stern's, Suaritos, Tapecar, Tico, Top Ten Hits, Top Hits, United Artists, UA Latino, Universal, Vaya, Verve, Virgin, Warner Brothers, Westminster, West Side Latino, World Circuit, World Pacific, Xenofile/Green Linnet. Any omissions or errors are unintentional and will be corrected in subsequent editions.

Que viva la musica